This book is provided to the

Presents of the
Commission on Independent Colleges
and Universities in New York

through the generosity of the attorneys in the
Higher Education Practice Group
at

Bond Schoeneck & King PLLC
at the

2017 Annual Meeting of CICU

Student Debt

Sandy Baum

Student Debt

Rhetoric and Realities of Higher Education Financing

Sandy Baum
The Urban Institute
Washington, DC, USA

ISBN 978-1-349-94943-4 ISBN 978-1-137-52738-7 (eBook)
DOI 10.1057/978-1-137-52738-7

Library of Congress Control Number: 2016946664

Cover illustration: Modern building window © saulgranda/Getty

Printed on acid-free paper

This Palgrave Pivot imprint is published by Springer Nature
The registered company is Nature America Inc. New York

Acknowledgments

A number of people provided comments that improved this book. I am grateful to Greg Acs, Steve Brooks, Martha Johnson, Jennifer Ma, Donald Marron, Michael McPherson, Saul Schwartz, and Patricia Steele for taking the time to help me think through the issues. Jennifer Ma also contributed invaluable editorial assistance. Any remaining errors are mine alone. The Urban Institute generously provided support for some of the time I devoted to this project.

My children, Benjamin, Daniel, Joshua, and Rachel Schwerin, give me the emotional support and the motivation that make my work possible. My husband, Michael McPherson, is infinitely patient and encouraging and, as always, provided intellectual insights and expertise critical to this book.

Contents

1 **Student Debt: Good, Bad, and Misunderstood** 1
A Student Loan Crisis? 4
Changes in Who Goes to College and Where They Go 9
It's Not a Simple Question of Good or Bad 10
Pinpointing the Problems 13
The Stories We Hear 2
Who Is in Debt? 7

2 **Student Loan Programs and the Realities of Student Debt** 17
The Basics of Policy Design 17
What Is the Purpose of Government Student Loans? 19
There Are Multiple Ways to Measure Student Debt 21
How Much do Individual Students Borrow? 22
How Much do Individuals Owe? 24
How Much Have College Graduates Borrowed? 25
Graduate Students Borrow Much More Than Undergraduates 27
How do Students' Borrowing Patterns Differ? 28
Older Students Borrow More Than Younger Students 28
Students Enrolled in For-Profit Institutions Borrow More Than Other Students 30
Each State Is Different 30

Why Has Student Debt Grown? 31
College Prices Have Risen Rapidly 31
Students also Borrow to Cover Living Expenses 32
Increases in Student Aid Have Softened the Impact of Rising Tuition 33
Most Incomes Have Not Grown, but Inequality Has 34
When Borrowers Don't Repay Their Debts 36
Too Many Borrowers Default on Their Student Loans 36
Insufficient Income Is Not the Only Possible Explanation for Not Making Payments 37
Default Rates Are Highest for Students from For-Profit Institutions and Community Colleges 38
Smaller Debts, Bigger Problems 38

3 Putting the Stories into Perspective 43
Media Sensationalism and the Development of the Common Wisdom 44
Policy Ideas Arising Out of the Panic 46
The Positive Impact of Student Loans 49
Society Benefits from Higher Education and so Does the Individual 50
Public Benefits Are Not the Same as Public Goods 52
Individual Decisions: Are Students Wrong to Incur Debt for College? 55
Going to College Leads to Higher Earnings 56
Everyone Doesn't Have the Same Great Outcome 58

4 The Evidence About the Impact of Student Debt 65
The Great Recession 66
Focusing on Total Outstanding Student Debt 66
What Is the Right Comparison? 68
It's Not Easy to Study the Impact of Student Debt 69
Studies of the Impact of Student Debt 70
Does Student Debt Stop People from Accumulating Wealth? 70
Does Student Debt Stop People from Starting Businesses? 71
Does Student Debt Stop People from Buying Houses? 73
Perceptions versus Reality 76
Student Debt and the Alternatives 78

5 How Can Public Policy Help? 83
Should Subsidizing Student Borrowers Be at the Top of the Social Agenda? 85
Preventing Problems 86
Excluding Institutions That Don't Serve Students Well 87
Helping Students Make Better Choices 88
A Comprehensive Strategy for Limiting Overborrowing 88
Is Information Enough? 90
Managing Existing Debt: Big Ideas 91
Improve Income-Driven Repayment 91
Make Repayment Easier 92
Don't Forgive All Student Debt! 93
Managing Existing Debt: Easier Fixes 94
Is Lowering All Interest Rates Really a Good Idea? 94
Don't Let So Much Unpaid Interest Accumulate 95
Don't Garnish Social Security Payments 96
Private Loans Should Not Be Called "Student Loans" 97
Treat Student Debt Like Other Debt in Bankruptcy 98
Provide Lines of Credit Instead of Preset Loan Amounts 98
Put Reasonable Limits on the Amounts Students and Parents Can Borrow 99
Don't Tax Forgiven Loan Balances 101
Improve Loan Servicing 101
Concluding Thoughts 102

References 107

Index 117

List of Figures

Fig. 1.1	Distribution of outstanding education debt by household income quartile, 2013	8
Fig. 2.1	Outstanding education debt in billions, 2003 to 2015	22
Fig. 2.2	Total federal and nonfederal borrowing in billions of 2014 dollars, 1994–95 to 2014–15	23
Fig. 2.3	Distribution of borrowers by amount of outstanding education debt, 2014	24
Fig. 2.4	Cumulative debt levels of bachelor's degree recipients in 2012 dollars over time	25
Fig. 2.5	Cumulative debt levels of associate degree recipients in 2012 dollars over time	26
Fig. 2.6	Average published and net tuition and fees and room and board at public four-year institutions in 2015 dollars, 1995–96 to 2015–16	33
Fig. 2.7	Share of aggregate income received by each fifth and top 5% of families over time	35
Fig. 2.8	Default rates by sector, 1995–96 to 2011–12	39
Fig. 2.9	Default rates for completers and noncompleters, 1995–96 to 2011–12	40

List of Tables

Table 2.1	Cumulative debt of 2011–12 bachelor's degree recipients	29
Table 2.2	Tuition and fees and room and board in 2015 dollars, 1985–86 to 2015–16	32
Table 2.3	Mean income received by each fifth and top 5% of families, in 2014 dollars	35
Table 2.4	Status of borrowers in repayment, 2014	37
Table 2.5	Student loan balances and five-year default rates	39
Table 3.1	Covering costs at public colleges and universities over time	51
Table 3.2	Median earnings by education level, 2014	57
Table 5.1	Enrollment of first-year undergraduate students by sector, 2011–12	100

CHAPTER 1

Student Debt: Good, Bad, and Misunderstood

Abstract Media anecdotes about individuals with student debt are unrepresentative and misleading. The general perception of a student debt "crisis" misses the reality that most education borrowing improves people's lives by increasing educational opportunities. Higher-income people carry more student debt than lower-income people. However, specific groups of people and specific types of debt cause serious difficulties. Finding solutions to the very real problems requires pinpointing the problems, targeting the solutions, and recognizing the responsibilities of both borrowers and taxpayers.

Keywords Student debt • College finance

> I am a member of the six figure debt club! I don't mind much though. Coming out of college, I was working two jobs, plus odd jobs and making close to $1000/month. I was on food stamps and constantly afraid of everything—a parking ticket or an especially cold month could put me over budget and prevent me from paying rent on time. I still have nightmares about it…
>
> Now, I make a stable, six figure salary working roughly the same hours—which, surprise, surprise, is more than 40 hours a week. But that's fine by me! I like working!
>
> Will I be paying off loans for the next 10–25 years? Yeah, but my life is so much better now than it was before taking on the debt to go to school.[1]

S. Baum, *Student Debt*, DOI 10.1057/978-1-137-52738-7_1

This online comment from a borrower is similar to the statement of a federal employee in Seattle quoted in a Zillow report who pays just over $1000 a month for debt from his bachelor's and master's degrees: "I think of it as a car payment," the borrower says. "Instead of a stupid car that's devaluating, it's a degree that helps me increase my income down the line. It's a car payment that's paying me back."[2]

But comments like these are not easy to find in the popular press. Anecdotes about individual students distressed by their student debt are much more common.

The Stories We Hear

A 2014 public radio story began with a young woman who earned a bachelor's degree from a public four-year university after transferring from a community college and graduated with $40,000 in debt.[3] What listener would guess that only about 12% of bachelor's degree recipients from public institutions graduate with this much debt—even though most spend all of their time at four-year institutions instead of starting at lower-price community colleges?[4] The article mentions that this young woman has deferred payment on her loans because her income is low. But it focuses more on her frustration that anyone expects her to be able to repay this debt.

Another borrower featured in this story earned a master's degree in history, with $110,000 in debt. This young man, the article notes, is in an income-driven repayment plan. In other words, he is not expected to make payments until his income exceeds 150% of the poverty level and then his payments will be a manageable percentage of his income above that level. But the article focuses on how overwhelmed he is by owing so much money.

Another story in the same public radio series gives an example of a young man who graduated from a highly selective private college in the Northeast with $30,000 of debt—a pretty typical debt level for bachelor's degree recipients who borrow. However, his dream is to be an organic farmer, so he makes only $12,000 a year (after taxes).[5]

These three examples, designed to elicit sympathy for the victims and anger at the position an unfair college financing system has put them in, reveal some significant problems—as well as some of the ways in which the student loan system increases opportunities for students. They also reveal some of the ways most public discussions of student debt obscure important realities.

Most common is the highlighting of individual students who are in unusual situations in a way that suggests that they are typical. In the first example above, as noted, the young woman is an outlier among bachelor's degree recipients. We don't know why she ended up borrowing so much. Perhaps she faced some hardship that made her situation particularly difficult; perhaps her parents were unwilling to contribute despite some ability to pay; perhaps she lived at a higher standard of living in college than many of her peers; perhaps she chose not to work for pay or was unable to find a job. In any case, she is quite likely to be able to manage her debt over the long run, particularly with all of the protections built into the federal student loan system.

The second example is of a graduate student. This is an important example, not because it is typical—only 7% of students who earned master's degrees in 2011–12 had borrowed as much as $110,000 for their undergraduate and graduate studies combined[6]—but because it highlights the problems of students making questionable decisions and of public policies that encourage these poor decisions. As detailed in later chapters, the restrictions on how much graduate students can borrow from the federal government are very loose. There are not many jobs that require master's degrees in history, and it is hard to imagine under what circumstances it would make sense to go $110,000 into debt to earn this degree. How can we prevent this situation from occurring? Even if it is rare, it should be unheard of.

The nation now has income-driven federal student loan repayment plans that will make life bearable for borrowers in this situation. But as a bachelor's degree holder, this borrower was hardly among the most vulnerable members of society when he made the decision to borrow. Under any reasonable income scenario, a significant portion of his debt will probably be forgiven—paid for by the taxpayers. Surely preventing the borrowing in the first place would be a better solution.

This reality leads to another characteristic of these examples and the way they are presented. One borrower is in deferment. This means that she has been allowed to postpone her payments because her income is inadequate. Another is in income-driven repayment and will never have to pay if he can't afford it. If the problem is that former students are overwhelmed with debt and the payments are making their lives difficult, how can it be that the fact that they are not actually being asked to make these payments is not at the center of the story?

What about the elite college graduate who wants to farm? His $30,000 in debt is not atypical. His choice—which he perceives as a right—to immediately follow a path that does not involve earning even a subsistence income certainly *should* be atypical. Who should pay for his elite education? Is it unrealistic to ask him to get an extra job or take a non-dream job for a few years to pay back the money he borrowed? Would he ever have thought about organic farming without his elite degree in environmental science?

A *New York Times* story, with a headline indicating that "Student Loans Make it Hard to Rent or Buy a Home," focuses on a young woman who "faced a daunting choice: pay rent or pay off her student debt."[7] She had taken out loans to put herself through four years at a public four-year university and couldn't—at first—find a job that would allow her both to pay basic living expenses and to make debt payments. She was apparently forced to be homeless. If, in fact, borrowers were expected to begin repaying their loans the day they graduated and there were no provisions for people facing financial hardship, many people probably *would* end up homeless for a while. But there is a six-month grace period before payments begin and, as already mentioned, there are options for deferring payments and for making payments proportional to income.

This list of examples—unlike the opening examples of borrowers saying that despite the unpleasant burden of repayment, life is much better than it would have been if they had not borrowed and gone to college—could go on and on. Headlines announce the intended message: "The Unforgiven: How College Debt is Crushing a Generation"[8] or "A Generation Hobbled by the Soaring Cost of College."[9] The latter article profiles a student who graduated from a private, church-related four-year university with $120,000 in debt and another who borrowed $80,000 to get her bachelor's degree in social work. Another dropped out of a for-profit institution with $100,000 in debt.

These examples are stunningly misleading about the circumstances of typical students. About 0.5% of 2011–12 bachelor's degree recipients—and 1% of those who earned their degrees at private nonprofit colleges—borrowed as much as $100,000; 1.5% overall and 3% from private nonprofit colleges borrowed as much as $80,000.[10]

A Student Loan Crisis?

It is largely stories like the more frequent and more visible ones cited above that have put the idea of a student loan "crisis" onto the national agenda. The idea of a student loan crisis has taken hold in the media, in the blogosphere, and in the political arena. But the reality is that borrowing for college is opening doors for many students. It is helping far more people than it is hurting.

There are some voices questioning the idea of a "crisis," but they are unlikely to be heard by a sizable segment of the population. With the same attention-getting headline style of articles making the opposing case, a *Forbes* article, "The Student debt crisis is being manufactured to justify debt forgiveness," points out that less than 20% of young families have student loan balances exceeding $8500 per adult. Only about 1% of households headed by a 20- to 40-year-old have a student loan balance over $50,000 per adult without a graduate degree to show for all that debt. In other words, most of those with big balances have the earning power to pay those loans off. "That does not sound like a crisis."[11]

Another *Forbes* column concludes that growing student debt levels are more related to the weak state of the economy than to rising college prices. Enrollment has grown; graduate students hold a very high percentage of the outstanding debt—about 40% of the total[12]; parents of traditional-age college students turned to student loans as the home equity and other savings they had counted on were undone by the market; and students and parents have realized that they can use lower-interest student loans to pay off higher-interest credit card debt.[13]

These isolated stories read only by a small segment of the public are not enough. It is time to rein in the general panic about student debt and find solutions to college financing problems that will make horror stories about borrowing for education more rare than they now are, ensure that as many people as possible have access to the education and training they need, and guarantee direct public support to those who really need it and can benefit most from it.

Perceptions of a student loan crisis, with student debt ruining the lives of former students and having a serious negative impact on the economy, are leading to wide-ranging proposals to relieve the debt burdens of any and all students. Proposals for forgiving all outstanding student debt and for guaranteeing debt-free college for future students aim to totally eliminate the concept of borrowing for college. According to proponents, student debt is a poison that must be eliminated if we are to have a healthy society. For example, #Million Student March organized protests at college campuses across the nation in November 2015 to call attention to their demands for cancellation of all student debt, in addition to tuition-free public college and a $15 minimum wage for all campus workers.[14]

This perception is not just overly simplistic. It is misguided and has the potential to significantly reduce educational opportunity in the USA. Even under the most optimistic scenario, where states increase their funding for higher education significantly and federal student aid becomes more and more generous, many people will be unable to go to college and complete degrees without borrowing. Young people from disadvantaged backgrounds and even from middle-income families, as well as older adults seeking to improve their lives, would be blocked from enrolling without access to credit. Borrowing for educational paths that are very likely to be dead end is a real problem. And some students borrow far too much. But borrowing is a reasonable option for many people seeking to invest in themselves and their futures.

Student debt *is* seriously harming too many former students. Some are borrowing without guidance about promising and suitable programs and institutions. Some are borrowing more than they really need to pay their tuition and support a basic lifestyle. Many aspects of the design of the allocation of student loans as well as the repayment and collection systems are in serious need of reform. States should revive their dwindling per-student funding to public colleges and universities that are partially responsible for increased borrowing and institutions should find ways to rein in costs without sacrificing quality.

But federal extension of credit to undergraduate students makes it possible for many individuals, particularly those with limited financial means, to go to college, to go to an appropriate college, and to succeed in college. Because of the positive impact of postsecondary education on employment and earnings, relatively affluent households carry a disproportionate amount of the outstanding student debt. Education borrowing is improving many more lives than it is damaging.

It is not borrowers with high levels of debt—most of whom have graduate degrees and very few of whom have less than a bachelor's degree—who are really struggling with student debt. Rather, it is those who borrowed relatively small amounts but did not emerge with educational credentials of value in the labor market. In other words, forgiving debt across the board or even lowering interest rates on that debt will provide the largest subsidies to people who don't really need the help. It will leave many who lack both the financial resources and the necessary guidance to succeed in the education system and the labor market without the support they need.

In a recent poll, 62% of respondents agreed with the idea that no one should borrow to pay in-state tuition—although only 46% thought the government should use tax revenues to cover the expenses.[15] Where will the money come from if not from taxpayers and not from students? A more analytical perspective clarifies why borrowing for college is a sensible idea. People have limited resources before they get an education, but that education is an investment that will boost their incomes over a lifetime. They can use part of the earnings premium to repay the debt. That's the same concept as borrowing to start a business.

The problem is not borrowing per se. It is borrowing for programs of study that are unlikely to pay off. It is borrowing more than can be justified by the expected payoff. And it is the uncertainty involved in the investment, which pays off very well on average and for most people, but not for everyone. Some of the outcomes are predictable and we should work to prevent the bad ones. Others are not predictable and borrowers need some form of insurance to protect against them.

Who Is in Debt?

The misperception that bachelor's degree recipients with very high levels of debt are typical coexists with the misperception that individuals who have borrowed for college are among the groups in society struggling most. In fact, because of the association between higher levels of education and higher incomes, education debt holders tend to be relatively well off.

As data from the Survey of Consumer Finances shown in Fig. 1.1 make clear, upper-income households carry a disproportionate amount of education debt, while lower-income households have less education debt than others. In 2013, the 25% of households with the highest incomes held 47% of all outstanding student debt. The 25% of households with the lowest incomes held 11% of the debt. Student debt is correlated with education and with earnings. The people who are having the most trouble making ends meet are those who have not gone to college and may not even have graduated from high school.

Twelve percent of adults over the age of 24 don't have a high school diploma or the equivalent and another 30% have no postsecondary experience.[16] These people have less earning power than people with college degrees, and in most cases less earning power than those with some college but no degree. If we want to target the worst-off people in society, it won't be through student debt relief.

The Occupy Wall Street movement provided a striking illustration of the socioeconomic realities underlying the depiction of student debt as a generalized crisis. Student debt was a central issue in the Occupy public communications. Efforts to eliminate student debt continue under the

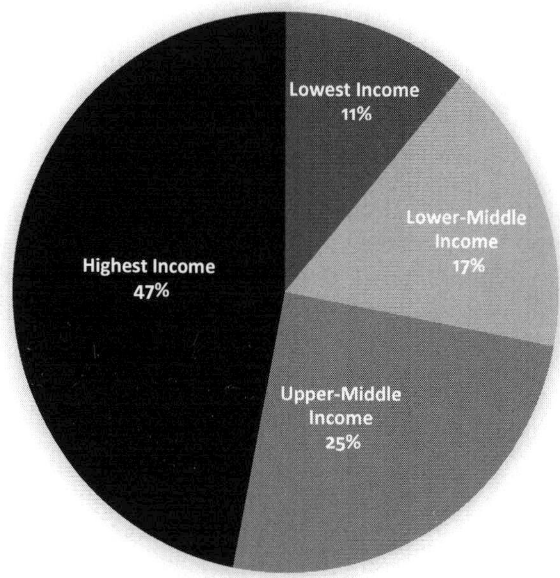

Fig. 1.1 Distribution of outstanding education debt by household income quartile, 2013
Note: Income quartiles are based on 2012 household income. The upper limits for the first three quartiles are: $25,000, $48,000, and $90,000
Source: Sandy Baum et al., *Trends in Student Aid 2015*, (New York: The College Board, 2015), Figure 19A. Based on data from the Survey of Consumer Finances

flag of the movement. But is student debt really a core concern of the least well-off members of our unequal society? Is this an issue around which the wide range of "99 percenters" could really unite?

The Daily Show's coverage of the movement highlighted reasons for skepticism.[17] Apparently, there was an "uptown" and a "downtown" within the protest movement. While middle-class activists, many carrying signs announcing the burden of their student debt, met for strategy meetings in the lobbies of bank buildings, another contingent was in an entirely different place. Homeless people, people with marginal attachment to the labor force, people without enough education to have taken student loans probably have different and more immediate needs at the tops of their lists.

This is not to suggest that student loans are not a problem for a significant number of individuals. It is not to suggest that no one who went to college is having difficulty finding a job paying a living wage. But in thinking about solutions to help these people, it is important to put their difficulties into context in order to develop constructive and progressive solutions.

Changes in Who Goes to College and Where They Go

Another central factor does not get enough attention in discussions of student debt. The population of college students has changed over time, along with the characteristics of the students borrowing to pay for college. It is not the population most casual observers would describe.

While there are people who could have gone to college 10 or 20 years ago without borrowing, but now find no other way to finance their education, it is also true that many more people now go to college than was the case a decade ago and certainly a generation ago.

In the late 1970s, less than one-third of high school graduates from the lowest family income quintile went straight to college. In the twenty-first century, more than half of this group starts college right after high school. (Immediate college-going went from about two-thirds to over 80% for those at the top of the income distribution.)[18]

During difficult economic times, when it is not easy to find a job, many people who would otherwise have gone straight to the labor force from high school, or who have been working for a while without a college degree, decide that the best option is to go back to school to strengthen their skills and increase their labor market opportunities.

Total postsecondary enrollment increased by 15% between 2007 and 2010. Of the 2.8 million new students, 837,000—30 of these new students—were enrolled in for-profit institutions. This sector accounted for about 7% of students in 2007 and 10% in 2010.[19] Students in this sector borrow significantly more than those with similar levels of education in the public and private nonprofit sectors. These students tend to be from lower-income backgrounds, to be older when they enroll, are disproportionately black and Hispanic, and have relatively low completion rates and weak labor market outcomes.

In 2000, only one of the 25 postsecondary institutions whose students held the largest amounts of outstanding debt was in the for-profit sector. At the top of the list were New York University (NYU) (private nonprofit) with $2.2 billion, the University of Phoenix (for-profit) with $2.1 billion, and Nova Southeastern University (NSU) (private nonprofit) with $1.7 billion. Fast forward to 2014. Of the top 25 schools, 13 were in the for-profit sector. The University of Phoenix topped the list with $35.5 billion in outstanding debt among students who last attended that institution. Walden University (for-profit) was second with $9.8 billion, followed by NSU at $8.7 billion. NYU, at $6.3 billion, had fallen to eighth place. The percentage of outstanding debt of the 25 highest-debt institutions held by the University of Phoenix jumped from 6% in 2000 to 21% in 2014. At 7 of the 25 highest-debt institutions—all in the for-profit sector—more than 40% of those who were supposed to begin repaying in 2009 had defaulted on their loans within five years. NSU and NYU, in contrast, had 6% default rates.[20]

In other words, the increase in student borrowing is not just about people who would have gone to college without borrowing 30 years ago now having to borrow. A big part of the story is about new subgroups of the population going to college and about a new set of institutions enrolling many of these students. A large number of these people come from middle- or lower-income families. Many are adults who are supporting themselves and sometimes their families. In fall 2013, 38% of all postsecondary students—and 31% of undergraduates—were age 25 or older.[21] A generation ago many of these people would not have gone to college at all. There were jobs available to high school graduates that provided living wages and job security. As that opportunity has faded, more and more of the job training in this country has moved into postsecondary institutions—colleges. People who would have gotten on-the-job training now go to college. They are part of all of the college financial aid programs—including student loans.

The student debt picture would look quite different if the only people at issue were the relatively privileged, mostly young people drawn from traditional college-going populations who went to college in the 1950s and 1960s.

It's Not a Simple Question of Good or Bad

Does it make sense to talk about student debt as a general phenomenon—something that is either good because it allows people with limited resources to invest in themselves or bad because it imposes too many burdens on students and signals that society doesn't really feel responsible for providing educational opportunities?

Many people would say that, in general, debt is a bad thing. If people borrow money, they are living beyond their means. But when it comes down to it, few people question the idea that borrowing to buy a house makes sense. In fact, concern over declining home ownership rates generates pressure to make mortgages more available to people of limited financial means. In the wake of the mortgage crisis, when it became obvious that many people had borrowed more than they could ever hope to repay and when many families lost their homes, no one is suggesting that borrowing to buy a house is a bad thing. Rather, guidelines for manageable debt are important. The terms of mortgages should not be exploitive. Consumers need better protection and there should be tighter control of the mortgage market. But we shouldn't either require that people pay up front for houses or make housing (which is certainly a fundamental need and right) free.

Some other examples of the problem with this sort of generalization may be helpful. Alcohol imposes very high costs on some individuals and on society. Some people's lives are ruined because they cannot control their alcohol consumption. Some people drive drunk and take the lives of others. We tried Prohibition. It's hard to argue that banning all alcohol consumption had worse consequences than banning borrowing for college—saying people could enroll only if they could pay up front—would have. Nonetheless, we quite reasonably modified the policy. Children are not allowed to buy alcohol. People are not allowed to drive under the influence. The reality that some people make bad decisions or are otherwise harmed by alcohol leads us to look for ways to solve the specific problems without depriving the majority of people, for whom alcohol plays a smaller but positive role in their lives, from enjoying this benefit.

There are few things that are good or bad for all people under all circumstances. Many people are concerned about the decline in the marriage rate. Marriage is a social institution with a very positive impact. It increases personal and financial security, provides children with more secure environments, and channels some anti-social tendencies. But clearly we should not advise young people just to get married because marriage makes life better. It matters when you get married, why you get married, and whom you marry.

Similarly, it matters when you go to college, why you go to college, and where you go to college. Some of the choices people make—and the options with which we present them—have predictable negative outcomes. No one should borrow money to go to a postsecondary institution with an abysmal graduation rate or poor job outcomes for those who do graduate. No one should put time and effort into such an institution even if it doesn't require borrowing. But that doesn't mean that all borrowing for college is bad. It just has to be cautious and well informed.

This book tries to sort through these nuances. Instead of talking about student debt as crippling, crushing, or hobbling a generation, let's find out where the real problems are and try to solve them.

Instead of sweeping and simplistic policy proposals, we should be focusing on the individuals and groups of individuals who are being harmed by our current student loan system. We know that high-risk students who enroll in for-profit institutions are much more likely to end up with unmanageable debt than are academically prepared students who enroll in public four-year colleges. We know that students who borrow for programs they are very unlikely to complete are most likely to default on their debts. We know that too many graduate students are borrowing very large sums to pursue occupations that will not generate the earnings required to repay their loans, while those who borrow even more for professional school are likely to successfully repay. We know that people who have experienced serious medical problems or who have trained for occupations later decimated by technology or by outsourcing are likely to struggle despite having made apparently good decisions about financing postsecondary education.

We do have a student debt problem that needs to be fixed. But it is not as general or as widespread as people believe. Overall, the availability of federal loans for college has increased educational opportunity and led to better lives for most borrowers. But too many students are making decisions about pursuing and financing postsecondary education without the guidance they need, leading to bad outcomes they could have avoided; too many students who have difficulty making payments face bureaucratic barriers to accessing the protections they need; too many borrowers are exploited by abusive collection procedures. We should improve the choices students make and the public policies that shape those choices. We should also carefully consider how responsibility for repaying education debt can and should be shared by individuals and society as a whole.

Pinpointing the Problems

Among borrowers who were supposed to begin repaying in 2011–12, 9% of those who completed a degree or certificate defaulted within two years. But a 24% default rate among those who left school without a credential brought the overall default rate up to 14%—a number that is rarely broken down in general discussions of the problem. Default rates among students who borrowed to attend public and private nonprofit four-year colleges were about 8%—compared to about 20% for those who borrowed to attend for-profit and public two-year institutions.[22]

Default is a separate problem from high levels of debt. Most of the 4% of borrowers carrying debts of $100,000 or higher will repay those debts—they have graduate degrees and relatively high earnings.

The typical borrower struggling with student debt is not the 22-year-old recent bachelor's degree recipient frequently pictured in news coverage. Rather, she is an older adult who either left school without completing her program or graduated with a short-term degree or certificate that may improve her circumstances, but not enough to provide a middle-class lifestyle.

We have to do a better job of pinpointing the problem, identifying its causes, and targeting potential solutions. That is the goal of this book.

Notes

1. Think Tank, July 16, 2015, comment on Darian Woods, "Medicine, Law, Business: Which Grad Students Borrow the Most?" *NPR Planet Money,* July 16,2015,http://www.npr.org/sections/money/2015/07/15/422590257/medicine-law-business-which-grad-students-borrow-the-most http://www.npr.octions/money/2015/07/15/422590257/medicine-law-business-which-grad-students- borrow-the-most.
2. Jamie Anderson, "Yes, First-Time Buyer Demand is Weak. But Stop Blaming Student Debt," *Zillow Real Estate Research*, September 16, 2015, http://www.zillow.com/research/student-debt-homeownership-10563/
3. Lucas Willard, "Part Seven of Student Loan Series: Sticker Shock," *WAMC*, December 22, 2014, http://wamc.org/post/part-seven-student-loan-series-sticker-shock.
4. Sandy Baum *et al.*, *Trends in Student Aid 2015* (New York: The College Board, 2015), Figure 17B.

5. Allison Dunne, "Part Five of Student Loan Series Focuses on Young Farmers," *WAMC,* December 19, 2014, http://wamc.org/post/part-five-student-loan-series-focuses-young-farmers.
6. NCES, National Postsecondary Student Aid Study 2012, Power Stats calculations. Thirty-one percent of 2011–12 master's degree recipients had no education debt and 50% borrowed less than $30,000.
7. Natalie Kitroeff, "Young and in Debt in New York City: Student Loans Make it Hard to Rent or Buy a Home," *New York Times,* June 6, 2014, http://www.nytimes.com/2014/06/08/realestate/student-loans-make-it-hard-to-rent-or-buy-a-home.html.
8. Jon Queally, "The Unforgiven: How College Debt is Crushing a Generation," *Common Dreams,* November 13, 2014, http://www.commondreams.org/news/2014/11/13/unforgiven-how-college-debt-crushing-generation.
9. Andrew Martin and Andrew Lehren, "A Generation Hobbled by the Soaring Cost of College," *New York Times,* May 12, 2012, http://www.nytimes.com/2012/05/13/business/student-loans-weighing-down-a-generation-with-heavy-debt.html?pagewanted=all.
10. NCES, National Postsecondary Student Aid Study 2012, Power Stats calculations.
11. Jeffrey Dorfman, "The Student Debt Crisis Is Being Manufactured To Justify Debt Forgiveness," *Forbes.* July 3, 2014, http://www.forbes.com/sites/jeffreydorfman/2014/07/03/the-student-debt-crisis-is-being-manufactured-to-justify-debt-forgiveness/.
12. Jason Delisle, *The Graduate Student Debt Review: The State of Graduate Student Borrowing* (Washington, DC: New America, 2014). p. 1.
13. John Ebersole, "The Unexamined Factors Behind the Student Debt 'Crisis'," *Forbes,* September 15, 2015, http://www.forbes.com/sites/johnebersole/2015/09/15/the-unexamined-factors-behind-the-student-debt-crisis/.
14. Curtis Skinner and Valerie Panne, "Students across U.S. march over debt, free public college," Reuters, November 12, 2015, http://www.reuters.com/article/2015/11/13/us-usa-college-protests-idUSKCN0T116W20151113#K4RfqD6rxHkPC4qY.97.
15. Peter Moore, "Three-fifths want taxes to fund debt-free college," *YouGov,* August 20, 2015, https://today.yougov.com/news/2015/08/20/three-fifths-want-debt-free-college/.
16. U.S. Census Bureau, *Current Population Survey*, 2014 Annual Social and Economic Supplement, Educational Attainment, Table 1, http://www.census.gov/hhes/socdemo/education/data/cps/2014/tables.html.
17. *The Daily Show with Jon Stewart*, October 18, 2011, http://www.cc.com/video-clips/5510me/the-daily-show-with-jon-stewart-occupy-wall-street-divided; November 16, 2011, http://www.cc.com/video-clips/409tf3/the-daily-show-with-jon-stewart-the-99-.

18. NCES, *Digest of Education Statistics 2014* (Washington, DC: U.S. Department of Education, 2015), Table 302.30.
19. NCES, *Digest of Education Statistics 2014*, Table 303.25.
20. Adam Looney and Constantine Yannelis, "A crisis in student loans? How changes in the characteristics of borrowers and in the institutions they attended contributed to rising loan defaults," *Brookings Papers on Economic Activity*, September 2015.
21. NCES, *Digest of Education Statistics 2014*, Table 303.45.
22. Adam Looney and Constantine Yannelis, "A crisis in student loans?"

CHAPTER 2

Student Loan Programs and the Realities of Student Debt

Abstract The main purpose of federal student loans is to solve cash flow problems, not to pay part of the cost of education. Grant aid is the best way to provide subsidies to disadvantaged students. But some borrowers need help paying back their loans because their education does not pay off as well as anticipated. Measures of the amounts individual students borrow are generally more meaningful than the total amount of debt outstanding and there is quite a bit of variation in the borrowing patterns of different students. For example, older students and graduate students tend to carry more debt than others. Default rates are disturbingly high, but the biggest problems are among students who do not complete their programs and among those who attended for-profit institutions.

Keywords Student debt • College finance • Student loan default

The Basics of Policy Design

The history of widely available student loans began in 1958 with the introduction of the National Defense Student Loan Program. In 1965, the Higher Education Act created the Guaranteed Student Loan Program, which made loans available to students by subsidizing banks to make the loans and guaranteeing that the federal government would repay the debts if the borrowers did not. The creation of Sallie Mae (The Student Loan

S. Baum, *Student Debt*, DOI 10.1057/978-1-137-52738-7_2

Marketing Association) as a government-sponsored corporation in 1972 was an effort to ensure the availability of credit by creating a secondary market for student loans. This organization has a checkered history. Its evolution into a for-profit company that has made many people wealthy at the same time that it has been accused of misleading and exploiting borrowers obscures its origin as an engine of opportunity for students.

The provisions of federal student loan programs and eligibility for those programs have varied over time. The basic pattern is that advocates lobby to expand the generosity of the programs. They succeed, but then the programs become more expensive than anticipated and Congress scales them back. For example, in 1978, the Middle Income Student Assistance program eliminated income restrictions for federal student loans. But after a few years, it became clear that paying the interest on all loans for all students while they were in school was not such a good idea.

The federal student loan program now in effect allows students to borrow regardless of their financial circumstances. The government pays the interest on Stafford Subsidized Loans, available in limited amounts to undergraduate students with documented financial need, while students are in school. Other loans accrue interest from the time they are issued.

Introduction of the PLUS loan programs, for parents in the 1980s and for graduate students in 2005, has also expanded federal lending. Unlike the Stafford federal student loan programs, the PLUS programs do not have specified limits on borrowing, but issue loans to cover any education-related expenses not covered by other financial aid. They are frequently cited as in need of reform.

Since 2010, when Congressional action eliminated the system of guaranteeing loans made by banks and other private lenders, all federal student loans are made directly by the federal government through the Direct Loan Program. But the history of federal education lending has led to a complicated and confusing set of programs facing today's borrowers.

Undergraduate students can borrow through the Stafford Subsidized and Unsubsidized federal student loan programs. Dependent undergraduates can borrow a total of only $31,000 in Stafford Loans over their years in school, but independent undergraduates can borrow up to $57,500—significantly more than five years of tuition and fees at the average public four-year college.[1] Because of the strict limits on annual borrowing, even borrowers with significant financial need usually rely on the loans that accrue interest from day one, in addition to Stafford Subsidized loans. The interest rates on these two types of federal loans have sometimes differed, but are now the same. They have at times been fixed by law at a particular interest rate, but now change annually depending on market rates—rates that are still fixed for the life of the loans.[2]

What Is the Purpose of Government Student Loans?

Paying part of the cost of education is not the core purpose of the student loan program. Other types of funding serve this important purpose. For example, we have public institutions of higher education, where taxpayers directly fund a portion of the costs. One reason we should and do subsidize students is because society as a whole benefits from postsecondary education. We will produce too little education if we don't pay collectively for the shared benefits. This is not the place to settle the critical question of exactly what the division of responsibility should be—but the decline in the portion covered by public funding in recent years is a serious problem that has certainly contributed to the increase in tuition at public institutions and to student debt levels.

In addition to this general funding for colleges and universities, equity considerations demand additional support for individuals with particularly limited resources. Some individuals are fortunate enough to have families able and willing to pay for much or all of the price of their education. For them, paying for college doesn't have to come out of their future earnings. Others are not so well situated. Expecting them to pay the whole price out of future earnings—even assuming their education generates the average high payoff—will put them at a permanent disadvantage. Too many will forgo college altogether because of the expense and others will carry very heavy debt burdens for years afterward.

A good way to provide this support designed to move us closer to a level playing field is by giving disadvantaged people the money to pay the bills when they come due. The system of need-based federal, state, and institutional grant aid is designed to do this.

In contrast, loans provide liquidity to pay for college—they help students finance their education at the time the bills come due. Unlike funding for institutions and grants to students that pay part of the cost of education, students have the responsibility to repay the loans later.

This does not mean, however, that there should be no subsidy at all in the loan program. Subsidies based on pre-college circumstances are best delivered through grant aid. But some subsidies should be designed to account for differences in post-college outcomes. As detailed in Chap. 3, the average payoff to a college education is quite high, but it varies quite a bit. Some of the variation is predictable, but much is not. Individuals from affluent backgrounds may enter socially valuable but low-paying occupations. Individuals from disadvantaged backgrounds may become wealthy. Anyone can suffer illness or disability or be unemployed in a weak economy. Financial assistance compensating for these differences can only be delivered after college, when they become apparent.

This variation in outcomes, both among individuals leaving school in any given year and across those graduating at different times into different economies, provides a strong argument for a loan system that adjusts expected payments to borrowers' incomes. The best design for such a policy is among the recommendations discussed in Chap. 5.

A more basic question about which there is some disagreement is whether and how much the overall loan system should involve subsidies. The student loan system could be designed to pay a part of the cost of education for all borrowers. Interest-free loans would be an example of this approach. Under this system, anyone who borrows, regardless of their financial circumstances before or after college, would benefit from subsidies from taxpayers. Because students who do not borrow would miss out on this funding, this type of system creates a strong incentive to borrow as much as possible and to postpone repayment for as long as possible.

At the other end of the spectrum, the system could be self-financing, with borrowers essentially paying for insurance that causes those with the best outcomes to subsidize those with the worst outcomes. Students who repay their loans in full in a timely manner would subsidize those who face difficulties, rather than having taxpayers take on this responsibility. A graduate tax, through which all former students finance education for current students—based on their incomes and without regard to how much support they received—is one model for this sort of system. A potential drawback to this approach is "adverse selection"—students who anticipate positive outcomes will hesitate to participate in the program, while those who expect to need help will be drawn to it.

A reasonable compromise is to limit the across-the-board subsidies—which are best delivered through general funding for all students, not just those who borrow—but to use the loan program to support those whose educations do not end up paying for themselves. Borrowers who reap the typical financial benefits from higher education repay their loans, preferably at interest rates that are lower than they would get in the private credit market, but high enough to make the system self-financing from the government's perspective. These borrowers would not bear the burden of compensating those for whom education doesn't work out so well. The cost of loan defaults or other payment problems would be borne by taxpayers in general, not just by the more successful borrowers. The insurance component of the program would be publicly funded, not the responsibility of only those who borrow for education.

This general principle does not settle all of the details of program design, but it does rule out some approaches. It means that we should not expect anyone to pay back more than they borrowed (including a reasonable rate of interest). It also means that we should not devote a lot of resources to minimizing interest rates across the board or forgiving debt so quickly or after such small expected payments that an unduly large proportion of borrowers never repay their debts. As discussed in Chap. 5, these criteria point to some modifications of the current system, particularly as it relates to graduate and professional students.

There Are Multiple Ways to Measure Student Debt

How Much Education Debt Is There?

The trillion-dollar student debt figure that begins many stories about the crisis refers to the total amount of education debt borrowed over time and not yet repaid. It includes loans made many years ago and those made last year. It includes both federal loans—those that come straight from the government and those made by private lenders and guaranteed by the federal government—and private loans made by banks and other lenders. It includes both parent and student loans, both undergraduate and graduate borrowing.

Figure 2.1 illustrates the Federal Reserve Bank of New York's data on outstanding student debt. It is easy to see from this graph that the total (not adjusted for inflation) keeps going up every year. It is a little harder to see that the rate of increase has actually declined. The largest one-year increases were in 2005 (40%) and 2006 (19%). The smallest increases were 7% in 2015 and 8% in 2004 and 2012. The largest three-year increase was 95% between 2004 and 2007; the smallest was 30% between 2010 and 2013.

The relatively small (by historical standards) percentage increases in outstanding debt in the most recent years result from a decline in the amount of borrowing during these years.

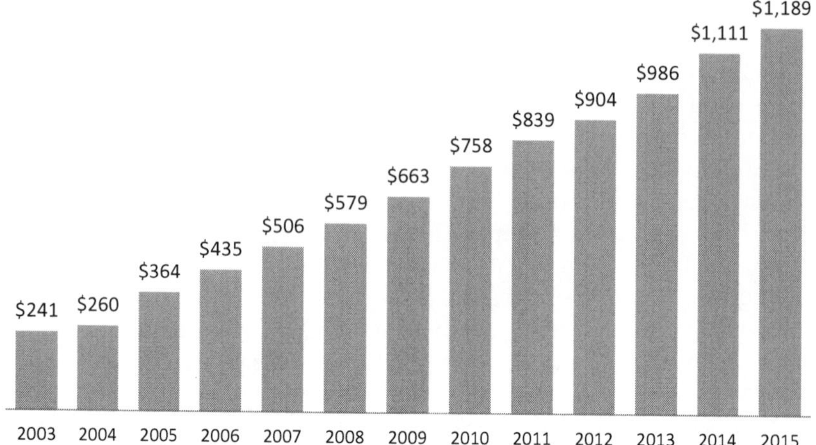

Fig. 2.1 Outstanding education debt in billions, 2003 to 2015
Note: Data are as of the end of the first quarter of the calendar year.
Source: Federal Reserve Bank of New York (2015), Quarterly Report on Household Debt and Credit

How Much do Individual Students Borrow?

Neither annual borrowing levels—overall or on average for individual students—nor the typical debt levels with which students graduate follow quite the same pattern as the aggregate outstanding education debt illustrated in Fig. 2.1. There is an overall upward trend in all of these, but both total annual borrowing and per-student borrowing have been declining for the past few years. These declines are not yet evident in either the total debt outstanding or the average debt of individual students.

As Fig. 2.2 illustrates, students and parents borrowed $91 billion in 2005–06, $124 billion in 2010–11, and $106 billion in 2014–15. Part of the recent decline is attributable to declining enrollment. As the economy has come out of the Great Recession, more people have chosen the labor market over college. Enrollment has particularly declined in the for-profit sector—the sector with the highest percentage of students borrowing. Changes in enrollment patterns affect both the total amount of borrowing and the composition of borrowers, with implications for how successfully the outstanding debt is likely to be repaid.

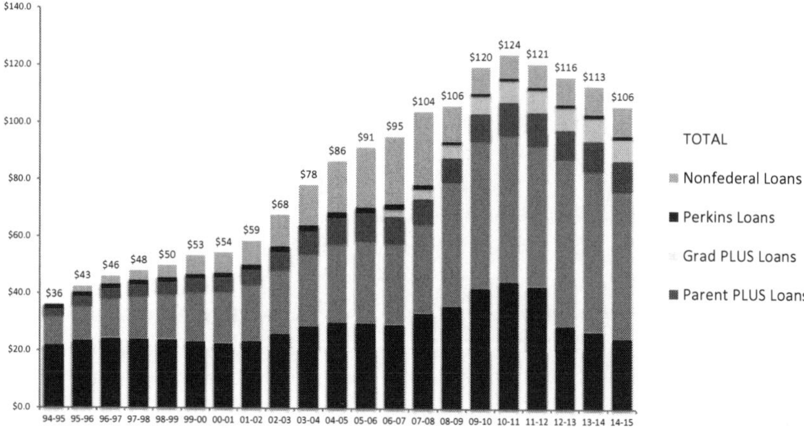

Fig. 2.2 Total federal and nonfederal borrowing in billions of 2014 dollars, 1994–95 to 2014–15
Source: Sandy Baum et al., *Trends in Student Aid 2015*, The College Board, Figure 5

But borrowing per student has also declined in recent years. Average federal loans rose from $4200 (in 2014 dollars) per full-time equivalent undergraduate student in 2004–05 to $5700 in 2010–11, but declined to $4800 in 2014–15. Federal loans per graduate student rose from $12,800 in 2004–05 to $18,700 in 2010–11, before declining to $16,600 in 2014–15.[3]

Looking only at those students who borrowed, in 2010–11, 9.4 million undergraduates borrowed an average of $6900 (in 2014 dollars) from the Stafford Unsubsidized and Subsidized Stafford Loan programs combined. In 2014–15, 8.3 million undergraduates borrowed an average of $6100. In 2010–11, 1.6 million graduate students borrowed an average of $23,900 from the Stafford and Grad PLUS federal loan programs. In 2014–15, 1.5 million graduate students borrowed an average of $22,900.[4]

In other words, discussions of trends in student debt must incorporate the recent decline in borrowing. The story has changed somewhat as the economy has come out of the depths of the downturn.

How Much do Individuals Owe?

The *New York Times* found a young woman who owes $220,000. She earned a bachelor's degree and started graduate school, but she works in a yogurt shop (or did when interviewed for the article) and is paid to drive an autistic child to and from school.[5] But as Fig. 2.3 illustrates, according to the Federal Reserve Bank of New York, less than 1% of borrowers with outstanding student loan debt owe as much as $200,000. Two-thirds owe less than $25,000. This woman's problems are very real, but they are not typical. She should have been prevented from—or at least strongly cautioned against—borrowing this extreme amount. The solution cannot be to allow students to borrow this way, with the most likely outcomes being either severe hardship for them or an inequitable burden on taxpayers.

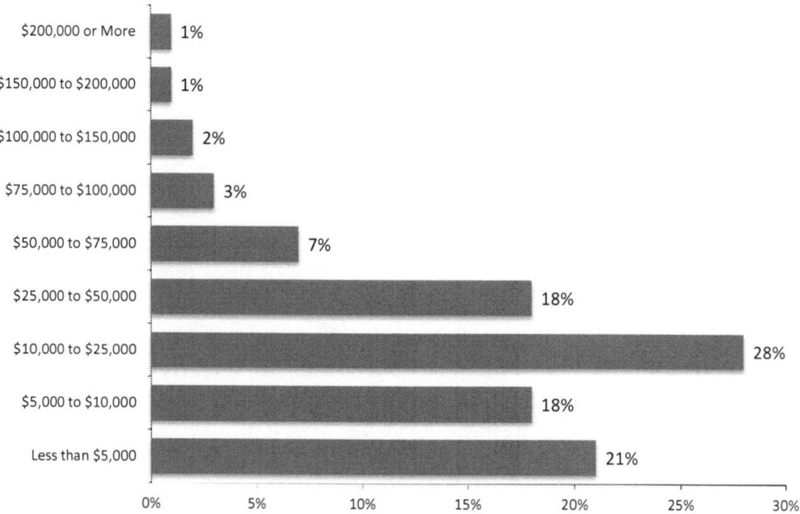

Fig. 2.3 Distribution of borrowers by amount of outstanding education debt, 2014

Note: Data are as of the end of the fourth quarter of 2014. Outstanding education debt includes borrowing by both students and parents for both undergraduate and graduate studies.

Source: Federal Reserve Bank of New York Consumer Credit Panel/Equifax

How Much Have College Graduates Borrowed?

The debt levels of students completing undergraduate degrees have increased markedly over time, but the patterns are quite different across types of institutions. Between 2003–04 and 2011–12, the percentage of bachelor's degree recipients who had borrowed $40,000 (in 2012 dollars) rose from 2% to 18%. The share of students with this level of debt increased in all sectors. But as Fig. 2.4 illustrates, the increase in public colleges and universities, which award almost two-thirds of all bachelor's degrees, was from 1% to 12%, while in the for-profit sector, which awarded 8% of bachelor's degrees in 2011–12, it was from 4% to 48%. These are large increases in the number of students with debt levels that could become difficult to manage for people whose labor market outcomes are below average for bachelor's degree recipients. They are debt levels that make careful monitoring of this growing minority of borrowers

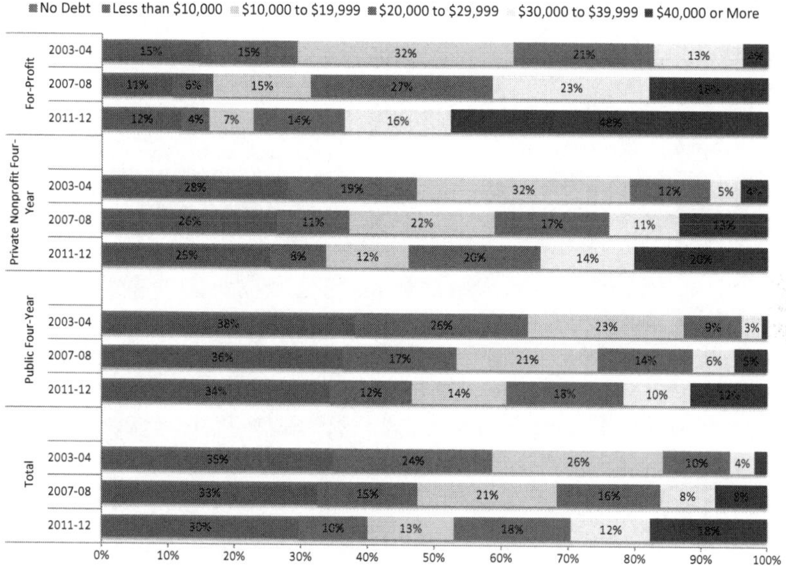

Fig. 2.4 Cumulative debt levels of bachelor's degree recipients in 2012 dollars over time

Note: The latest data available for individual students are for 2011–12. Includes both federal and nonfederal borrowing.

Source: Sandy Baum, Diane Elliott, and Jennifer Ma, *Trends in Student Aid 2014*, The College Board. Based on data from NCES, National Postsecondary Student Aid Study 2012

critical. That said, 30% of bachelor's degree recipients graduated without education debt in 2011–12 and another 23% borrowed less than $20,000. Again, high debt levels are not typical.

Associate degree recipients borrow less than students earning four-year degrees. They are typically in school for a shorter period of time, and many of them attend community colleges, which have lower tuition and fees than four-year institutions, where they often enroll part time. But even among these students, debt levels have risen considerably.

The percentage of associate degree recipients graduating with $20,000 (in 2012 dollars) or more in debt increased from 1% in 2003–04 to 8% in 2011–12. But for those from the for-profit sector, which awarded 20% of associate degrees in 2011–12, the increase was from 1% to 28%. In contrast, among the three-quarters of 2011–12 associate degree recipients who graduated from public two-year colleges, 59% had no education debt and 4% borrowed $30,000 or more. Associate degrees do not generally lead to earnings as high as bachelor's degrees, so it makes sense to be concerned about lower levels of debt for these individuals than for those with higher levels of educational attainment (Fig. 2.5).

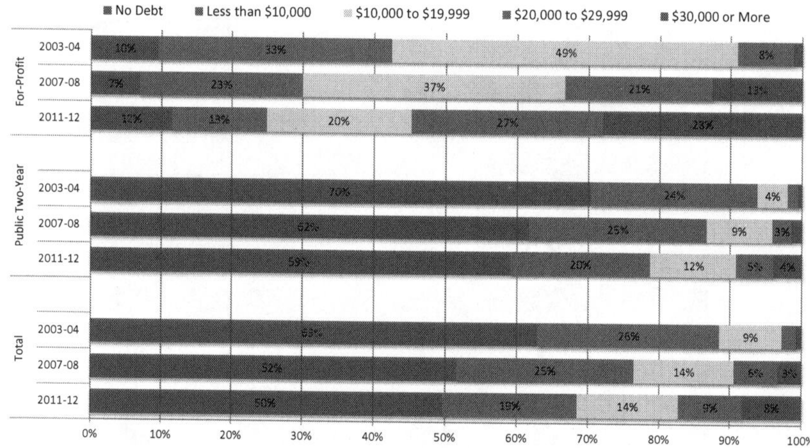

Fig. 2.5 Cumulative debt levels of associate degree recipients in 2012 dollars over time

Note: The latest data available for individual students are for 2011–12. Includes both federal and nonfederal borrowing.

Source: Sandy Baum, Diane Elliott, and Jennifer Ma, *Trends in Student Aid 2014*, The College Board. Based on data from NCES, National Postsecondary Student Aid Study 2012

Graduate Students Borrow Much More Than Undergraduates

The majority of borrowers with very large debt balances went to graduate school. In 2011–12, when about 20% of the degrees completed were graduate degrees, two-thirds of the students graduating with $50,000 or more in debt—and 94% of those with $100,000 or more in debt—had completed master's or doctoral degrees.[6]

Graduate students can borrow as much as $138,500 from the Stafford Loan program that serves both undergraduate and graduate students. And if that is not enough, they can borrow up to the full cost of attendance—tuition, fees, room, board, books, supplies, transportation, and other expenses not covered by financial aid—from the Plus Loan program for as many years as they are enrolled.

Sixteen percent of graduate students who completed their programs in 2011–12 (and 22% of those who borrowed) had accumulated $100,000 or more in debt. Among those receiving professional practice degrees such as law and medicine, 62% overall and 72% of those who borrowed had this much debt.

These funds don't just cover the price of education. These are funds on which graduate students and their families can live for a number of years. Balancing the availability of credit to foster educational opportunity with limits to prevent levels of borrowing that are both unintended lifestyle subsidies and risk factors for post-education well-being is a challenge.

The average cumulative amount borrowed by students receiving professional degrees in law and medicine in 2011–12 was about $130,000. Perhaps of greater concern, debt among master's degree students is high and growing in some fields that rarely lead to the kind of earnings doctors, lawyers, and MBAs might expect. Eighteen percent of 2011–12 master's degree recipients had accumulated $80,000 or more in debt for their undergraduate and graduate studies combined—up from 2% (measured in 2012 dollars) eight years earlier.[7]

Law student debt has garnered quite a bit of attention recently, as the job market for lawyers has weakened. Lawyers' earnings vary dramatically depending on their specific occupations and are highly correlated with the prestige of the law school a student attended.[8] Too many students are borrowing too much for law school and the public policies supporting this borrowing require attention, as discussed further in Chap. 5.

Some graduate student debt is surely a problem, but the people taking the loans are in very different circumstances than those borrowing for undergraduate study and in most—although certainly not all—cases, their earnings are likely to support the debt.

The policy considerations relating to graduate students are quite different from those relating to undergraduates. The individuals incurring this debt already have bachelor's degrees and are among those in the labor force with the highest earnings potential. They are also older and more educated than most people making decisions about undergraduate debt. Despite their high debt levels, graduate borrowers have relatively low default rates. Among all undergraduate and graduate borrowers who were supposed to begin repaying in 2010, a startling 28% overall defaulted within five years. The rate was lower for those borrowing to attend selective colleges—10%—and it was 5% for those who had only graduate school debt.[9] Chapter 5 returns to this issue.

How do Students' Borrowing Patterns Differ?

The data on borrower debt levels make it very clear that an increasing share of students are borrowing at levels that could be challenging if they are at the lower end of the earnings distribution for their types of degrees—and if the repayment protections including deferment of payments for borrowers with low incomes and income-driven repayment plans attached to federal student loans do not provide the needed relief. But the data also make it clear that most college graduates—and even most of those graduating with debt—are not in this situation.

One of the difficulties with talking about a "student debt crisis" is that it fails to differentiate among students with different characteristics in different circumstances. If, in accord with a central argument of this book, borrowing for college is not a bad thing per se, we must look at categories of students and find out where the real problems lie.

Table 2.1 displays the distribution of cumulative debt for 2011–12 bachelor's degree recipients with different characteristics.

Older Students Borrow More Than Younger Students

Most stories about student debt focus on people in their early twenties struggling to establish themselves as adults. While this population is consistent with the standard image of college students, many students are considerably older. These older students tend to borrow more than traditional-age college students and have lower completion rates. For example, among students who first enrolled in college in 2008 when they

Table 2.1 Cumulative debt of 2011–12 bachelor's degree recipients

	No Debt	Less than $10,000	$10,000 to $19,999	$20,000 to $29,999	$30,000 to $39,999	$40,000 or More
			Age at Completion			
23 or Younger (60%)	34%	12%	14%	19%	11%	11%
24 to 29 (20%)	21%	12%	12%	15%	14%	25%
30 to 39 (11%)	21%	6%	11%	15%	14%	33%
40 or Older (9%)	30%	5%	10%	13%	13%	29%
			Dependency Status			
Dependent (56%)	34%	12%	14%	19%	10%	11%
Independent, No Dependents (25%)	25%	9%	12%	15%	13%	25%
Independent with Dependents (19%)	23%	8%	10%	15%	15%	29%
			Time Elapsed Between First Enrollment and Degree Completion			
Within 4 Years (39%)	36%	11%	15%	19%	9%	10%
5 Years (21%)	29%	11%	12%	19%	13%	15%
6 Years (10%)	25%	11%	12%	19%	16%	17%
7 to 9 Years (12%)	23%	11%	12%	13%	13%	28%
10 Years or Longer (19%)	24%	6%	10%	15%	14%	31%
			Sector			
Public Four-Year (56%)	34%	12%	14%	17%	10%	12%
Private Nonprofit Four-Year (26%)	25%	8%	12%	20%	14%	20%
For-Profit (9%)	12%	4%	7%	14%	16%	48%
Other (8%)	28%	11%	14%	16%	11%	20%
			Race/Ethnicity			
Asian (6%)	43%	12%	14%	17%	7%	7%
Black (12%)	14%	11%	12%	16%	15%	32%
Hispanic (12%)	27%	11%	14%	17%	14%	17%
White (66%)	32%	10%	13%	18%	12%	16%
Total	30%	10%	13%	18%	12%	18%

Source: Baum et al., *Trends in Student Aid 2015*, The College Board.

were age 20 or younger, 59% had completed a credential six years later, compared to about 40% of those who were older when they started college.[10] Only 11% of students who completed bachelor's degrees in 2011–12 when they were age 23 or younger had borrowed as much as $40,000, but about 30% of those who completed their degrees at age 30 or older had accumulated this much debt.[11] They should be a focus of any investigation into problems in our higher education financing system.

Students Enrolled in For-Profit Institutions Borrow More Than Other Students

Older students—and low-income traditional-age college students—are overrepresented in postsecondary programs and institutions that are very different from the classic image of an ivy-covered college or university campus, where most students spend four (or five or six) years studying for a bachelor's degree and much of that time living in a dormitory on campus. Despite repeated complaints that too many people are being urged to go to college when they should instead be seeking occupational training, the reality is that data on college enrollment include anyone enrolled in any post-high school educational or training institution. Over half of the undergraduate degrees awarded in 2012–13 were short-term certificates or associate degrees, not bachelor's degrees.[12] And of particular importance for our purposes, student loans fund all types of postsecondary education. Thirty percent of federal student loans go to students enrolled in either community colleges or for-profit institutions.[13]

In 1970, 73% of postsecondary enrollment was in four-year institutions and 23% was in two-year institutions. By 1990, the breakdown had changed to 62% and 38% and in 2013 it was 66% in four-year and 34% in two-year institutions. Less than 1% of enrollments were in for-profit institutions until 1981, but this sector reached 3% in 2000, 6% in 2005, and 10% in 2010. In 2013, 8% of enrollments were in the for-profit sector.[14] This evolution means that "traditional" college students are a smaller fraction of the total than they once were—and a smaller fraction than people imagine when they talk about the generic student debt problem.

Each State Is Different

National averages tell important stories, and most student loan policies are made in Washington. But both broader higher education policies and economic opportunities vary dramatically across states. For example, in 2015–16, average tuition and fees at public four-year colleges and universities range from $4900 in Wyoming and $6400 in Montana to $15,000 in Vermont and $15,200 in New Hampshire.[15] Six states provided less than $100 per full-time equivalent undergraduate student in grant aid to help students pay for in-state colleges in 2013–14, while another 11 provided more than $1000 per student.[16] Some states focus on providing funding for students with the highest financial need, while others focus on rewarding students with strong test scores or high school grades.

Students from similar backgrounds pursuing similar educational paths will pay very different prices and probably accumulate very different amounts of debt depending on where they live. Their ability to pay off that debt will also vary depending on the employment opportunities and the cost of living in their area of residence after college.

Why Has Student Debt Grown?

The passionate opposition to student debt did not come out of nowhere. The total amount of outstanding student debt, the total amount students borrow each year, and the average amounts individual students borrow have all risen rather dramatically over the past decade. And the weak economy, which has made it more difficult for graduates (and those who do not graduate) to find well-paying jobs, has made this growing debt more of a problem for more people. It has also obscured the very real long-term rewards that do and will accrue to most of the people who have borrowed for college.

College Prices Have Risen Rapidly

There are a number of reasons why this has happened. One is certainly the rapid rise in college tuition prices. This is not a new phenomenon. College prices have been rising faster than average prices in the economy for decades. As Table 2.2 shows, across the nation as a whole, public four-year college tuition and fees increased by 51% between 1985–86 and 1995–96 and by 52% between 1995–96 and 2005–06, after adjusting for inflation. Over the most recent decade, the increase was smaller—but still 40% larger than the increase in the Consumer Price Index over these ten years. Room and board charges have gone up more slowly, but still much faster than average prices of goods and services.

Table 2.2 Tuition and fees and room and board in 2015 dollars, 1985–86 to 2015–16

	Tuition and Fees in 2015 Dollars			Tuition and Fees and Room and Board in 2015 Dollars	
Academic Year	Private Nonprofit Four-Year	Public Four-Year	Public Two-Year	Private Nonprofit Four-Year	Public Four-Year
1985–86	$13,600	$2,900	$1,400	$19,700	$8,500
1990–91	$17,100	$3,500	$1,700	$24,700	$9,300
1995–96	$19,100	$4,400	$2,100	$27,200	$10,600
2000–01	$22,200	$4,800	$2,300	$30,700	$11,700
2005–06	$25,600	$6,700	$2,700	$35,100	$14,800
2010–11	$29,300	$8,400	$3,000	$39,900	$17,700
2015–16	$32,400	$9,400	$3,400	$43,900	$19,500
1985–86 to 1995–96	40%	52%	50%	38%	25%
1995–96 to 2005–06	34%	52%	29%	29%	40%
2005–06 to 2015–16	27%	40%	26%	25%	32%
2005–06 to 2010–11	14%	25%	11%	14%	20%
2010–11 to 2015–16	11%	12%	13%	10%	10%

Source: Ma et al., *Trends in College Pricing 2015*, The College Board, Table 2.

Students also Borrow to Cover Living Expenses

Published prices at colleges and universities are by no means the whole story. One issue is that tuition—especially tuition net of grant aid—represents a small part of the expenses for which college students borrow. In 2015–16, tuition and fees (before grant aid) range from 20% of the total budget for public two-year college students living off campus to two-thirds of the total for private nonprofit four-year college students living on campus.[17] Lower tuition, or even free tuition, won't change the living expenses students pay—frequently with money they borrow—while they are in school.

A sobering example relates to veterans who go back to school. The post-9/11 GI bill covers four years of tuition at public universities for most of these students and also provides a generous living allowance. Yet a significant number of veterans receiving these benefits also take out federal loans. According to the *Los Angeles Times*, 26% of the veterans receiving these benefits in 2012 borrowed an average of $7400.[18] When the money is available, it is not difficult to find ways to spend it. The problem is not just the price of college, but some combination of the struggles people face in meeting basic living expenses for themselves and their families and the temptation to go beyond those basic expenses, with inadequate recognition of the implications for the future.

Increases in Student Aid Have Softened the Impact of Rising Tuition

Also critical to understanding the role of college prices is that most students don't actually pay these published prices. Instead, they get grants and scholarships from federal and state governments, from their colleges and universities, and from employers and other sources. Federal education tax credits, which are delivered long after tuition bills are due, also provide significant subsidies to students and families.

The net tuition prices that students pay are lower and have grown more slowly over time than the published prices. As Fig. 2.6 reveals, on average, the net prices students paid at public four-year institutions actually

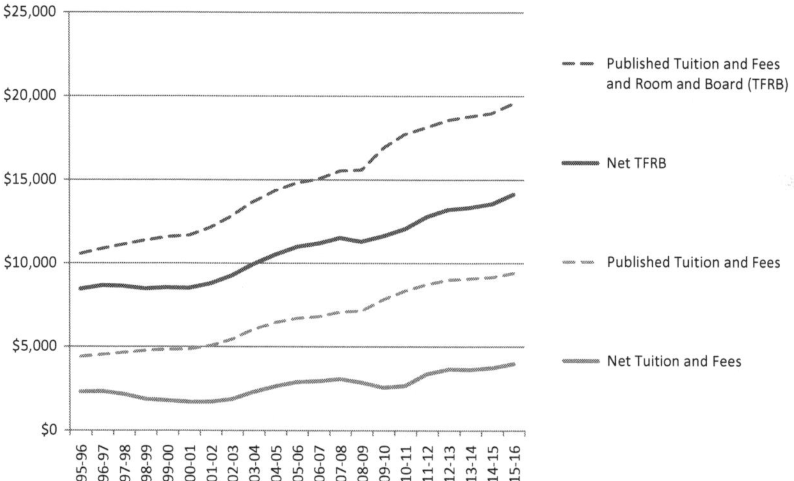

Fig. 2.6 Average published and net tuition and fees and room and board at public four-year institutions in 2015 dollars , 1995–96 to 2015–16
Source: Jennifer Ma et al., *Trends in College Pricing 2015*, The College Board, Figure 12)

declined in inflation-adjusted dollars between 2007–08 and 2010–11. This happened because in the depths of the recession, the federal government stepped in to ameliorate the problems students and families faced as state budget cuts led to rapid price increases at public colleges; plunging endowment values and annual giving put pressure on private colleges; and high unemployment, declining wages, and evaporating home equity and other savings made paying for college a real challenge.

Congress and the Administration worked together to double the funding distributed to low- and moderate-income students through the Pell Grant program between 2008–09 and 2010–11and also implemented the American Opportunity Tax Credit (AOTC). Providing subsidies of up to $2500 per student, the AOTC replaced a less generous tax credit and, with the addition of partial refundability to benefit students and families with no tax liability, led to a dramatic increase in the extent to which the federal government uses the tax system to help people pay for college.

Most Incomes Have Not Grown, but Inequality Has

At least as important as college prices in understanding student debt patterns are the trends in family incomes and in who goes to college. How difficult it is to pay for this major undertaking depends not only on how much it costs, but also on the resources available to pay for it.

The rising price of college is a more serious issue because of the failure of incomes to keep up. As Table 2.3 indicates, the average income for families in the middle of the income distribution and below was lower after adjusting for inflation in 2014 than it had been in 2004. Families at the upper end of the income distribution saw small increases over the decade. Over the 30 years from 1984 to 2014, incomes at the bottom did not grow, average income for the middle group increased by 16% ($9200 in 2014 dollars), and average income for the top fifth of families rose by 51%. The $73,700 increase for this group was larger than the 2014 average income of $66,900 for families in the middle.

Rising income inequality, as illustrated in Fig. 2.7, means that people at the top can manage rising prices much better than people in the middle, and that people at the bottom struggle more and more just to make ends meet. It also increases the stress and pressures facing families who are not at the top of the distribution, as they view the lifestyles of others, confront more unattainable consumption opportunities, and have a general sense that their financial well-being is deteriorating. Families in the top fifth of

Table 2.3 Mean income received by each fifth and top 5% of families, in 2014 dollars

Year	Lowest Fifth	Second Fifth	Third Fifth	Fourth Fifth	Highest Fifth	Top 5 Percent
2014	$16,100	$40,700	$66,900	$103,100	$217,000	$370,100
2004	$17,800	$42,400	$68,000	$101,600	$211,400	$368,300
1994	$16,400	$38,900	$61,400	$90,700	$182,800	$313,600
1984	$16,300	$37,400	$57,700	$82,500	$143,400	$207,300
2004 to 2014	–10%	–4%	–2%	1%	3%	0%
1994 to 2014	–2%	5%	9%	14%	19%	18%
1984 to 2014	–1%	9%	16%	25%	51%	79%

Source: U.S. Census Bureau (2015), Income Table F-3.

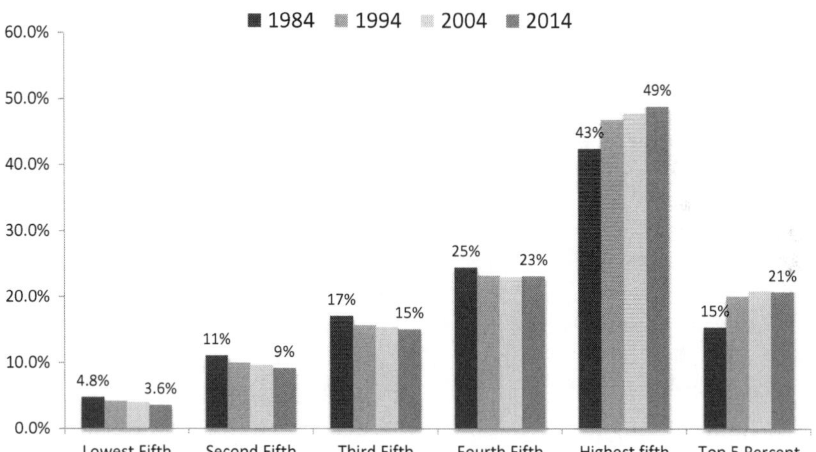

Fig. 2.7 Share of aggregate income received by each fifth and top 5% of families over time
Source: US Census Bureau (2015), Income Table F-2

the income distribution have done very well relative to those below them. But the gap between most of them and those at the very top (like the much-discussed 1%) has grown, changing the way they perceive their own opportunities and constraints.

Over years when more parents of college students who are recent high school graduates have been unemployed or suffered income declines and older college students have had more difficulty finding jobs that can help them support themselves and their families while they are in school, it is not surprising that student loans have picked up some of the slack.

When Borrowers Don't Repay Their Debts

Borrowers who do not make the required payments on their student loans for 270 days are in default. People who default on auto loans lose their cars. Many people who defaulted on their mortgages during the housing crisis lost their homes. It is not possible to repossess an education, but default on student loans is a serious problem. It is a problem for taxpayers, who end up arbitrarily providing significant subsidies to a variety of individuals, some of whom may be appropriately targeted because of the difficulties they face. Others, however, may have borrowed without the intention to repay or may have simply decided that repaying was not a high priority. The consequences for individuals, however, are most serious.

While it takes nine months of delinquency for a loan to actually be considered in default, once that happens the federal government has many tools at its disposal for collecting the debt—and for punishing the borrowers who have not met the terms of their loan contracts. Borrowers may incur very high collection charges, which can be added to the principal along with unpaid interest. The government can garnish wages or confiscate tax refunds to collect on the debt. Defaults are reported to credit agencies, so defaulters are likely to have difficulty accessing credit, renting an apartment, or even getting a job.

Too Many Borrowers Default on Their Student Loans

The official federal student loan three-year default rate released in 2015 was 12%. This is the percentage of borrowers who should have begun making loan payments in 2011–12 who defaulted by the end of 2013–14. It represents a decline from 15% two years earlier.[19]

As Table 2.4 reports, in 2014 only 29% of borrowers in repayment were always current and had decreasing balances. Some of the loans of borrowers taking advantage of provisions that allow them to postpone

Table 2.4 Status of borrowers in repayment, 2014

	Percentage of total
Always current, balance decreasing	29%
Always current, balance increasing	34%
Current with previous blemish	20%
Now delinquent	6%
Now in default	11%
Total borrowers in 2014:Q4	100%

Source: Haughwout et al., "Student Loan Borrowing and Repayment Trends, 2015," Federal Reserve Bank of New York

their payments on federal student loans because their current incomes are inadequate are not required to make any payments. Some who are enrolled in income-driven repayment plans may be making payments that are too small to cover the interest charges. Accordingly, even borrowers in good standing may not be paying down their balances, and some may be seeing their balances grow as interest accrues. It is good policy to let borrowers postpone their payments until they can afford them, but the startlingly low percentage of former students who are successfully retiring their debts clearly demands attention.

Insufficient Income Is Not the Only Possible Explanation for Not Making Payments

In addition to objective financial constraints, attitudes and priorities affect how borrowers approach loan repayment. Lost in most of the discussion of the oppressive burden of student loans is the reality that we all make choices about how to spend our finite resources. Many observers—and many borrowers as well—view student loan payments as an add-on to all consumption and to other obligations. It is the student loan payments that put people over the edge. But recognizing that it is the education financed by student loans that makes the income for other expenses available should raise questions about that perspective.

It is not easy to define "necessities" and no one can prescribe priorities for others. Some people would rather live in their parents' basement and have the opportunity to travel, while others would choose a fancy apartment over being able to eat out or buy nice clothing. The too rare testimonials of borrowers who prioritize paying off their education debts as rapidly as possible reveal the different sacrifices people choose to make when they understand the importance of tackling this debt. A recent *Forbes* article described a married couple living off of one salary while using the other to pay down student debt; a young man who gave up his own apartment to live with a roommate and is postponing adding expensive vacations to his lifestyle; and another borrower who moved in with his parents and stopped spending so much on entertainment.[20]

Should people have to live at a reduced standard of living after college in order to pay off their debts? It is obvious that individuals with student debt will be unable to save and consume as much as similar individuals with the same incomes and no debt. It is certainly reasonable to argue that it is unfair that some people have parents who can pay for college and others don't. Much of our federal, state, and institutional financial aid systems are designed to mitigate these differences. But they will never equalize options, particularly as long as the level of inequality in our society is so high and continuing to grow.

Default Rates Are Highest for Students from For-Profit Institutions and Community Colleges

The 12% default rate cited above conceals very different default rates for borrowers from different types of institutions: 6% for private nonprofit four-year colleges, 8% for public four-year colleges, 16% for for-profit institutions, and 19% for community colleges.[21] To put these figures into perspective, it is important to note that borrowing is more prevalent at some types of institutions than at others. In 2011–12, when 42% of all undergraduate students took loans, only 18% of community college students borrowed. In contrast, about 70% of those attending for-profit institutions borrowed.[22]

As illustrated in Fig. 2.8, default rates among students who borrowed to attend for-profit and two-year public institutions are consistently almost three times as high as the rates among students from four-year public and private nonprofit colleges and universities. Again, it is not the traditional college students frequently making the front page of the newspaper, but the nontraditional students—likely older, independent, seeking occupational preparation—that are most likely to encounter repayment problems.

Smaller Debts, Bigger Problems

Notably, it is not borrowers with high levels of debt who are most likely to default. Rather, as Table 2.5 shows, default rates are highest for those with the lowest levels of debt.

Many borrowers who owe just a few thousand dollars were in school for just a short period of time. They may be struggling with their debt because they did not complete the investment in education necessary to get a real payoff in the labor market—a better job and higher earnings.

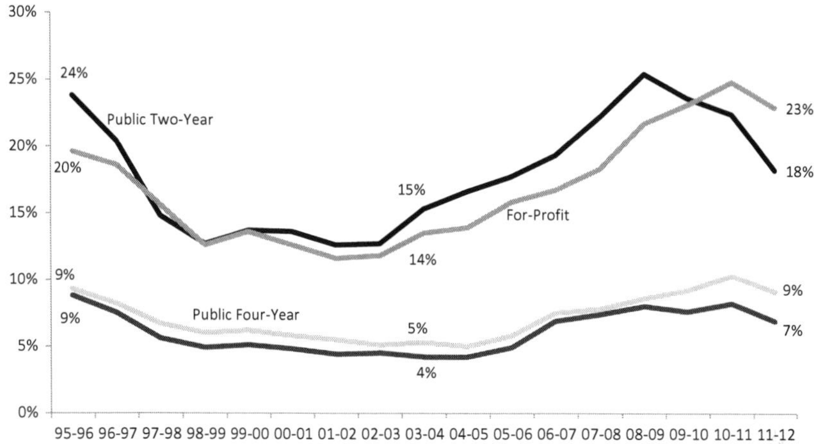

Fig. 2.8 Default rates by sector , 1995–96 to 2011–12
Source: Baum et al., Trends in Student Aid 2015, The College Board, Figure 12. Based on data from U.S. Department of Treasury.

Table 2.5 Student loan balances and five-year default rates

Debt Balance Upon Leaving School	Percentage Who Defaulted by 2014, Fourth Quarter
Less than $5000	34%
$5000 to $10,000	29%
$10,000 to $25,000	24%
$25,000 to $50,000	21%
$50,000 to $100,000	21%
$100,000 or More	18%

Source: Brown et al., *Looking at Student Loan Defaults Through a Larger Window*, The Federal Reserve Bank of New York

Perhaps the most consistent and striking finding about student loan defaults is the role of degree completion. Studies of the factors influencing default have long shown that not completing a credential is the strongest predictor of nonpayment. The Treasury Department's recent analysis of data from the National Student Loan Data System, shown in Fig. 2.9, makes the differences in default rates concrete. Among borrowers who

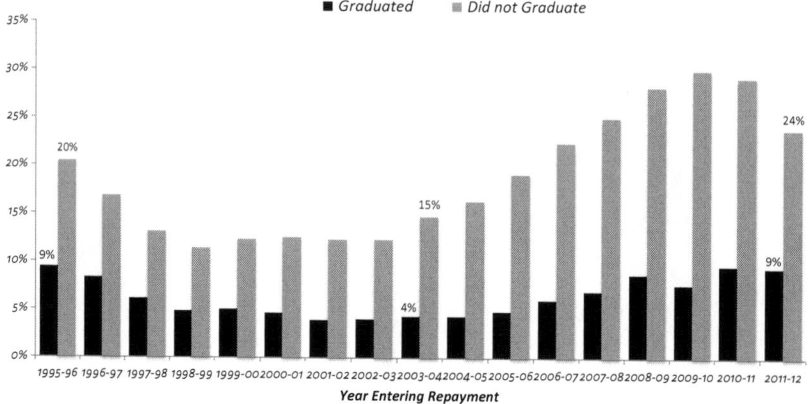

Fig. 2.9 Default rates for completers and noncompleters , 1995–96 to 2011–12
Source: Baum et al., Trends in Student Aid 2015, The College Board, Figure 14A. Based on data from the U.S. Department of Treasury.

were supposed to begin repaying in 2011–12, 24% of those who had not completed a degree or certificate had defaulted within two calendar years, compared to 9% of those who graduated. The overall default rate is disconcertingly high, but hides very important information about who is likely to repay their student loans and who is not.[23]

The default rate on student loans is cause for real concern. A system that puts many people into this situation needs repair. It is also important to remember that when borrowers fail to repay their federal student loans, if the government never recovers the money, taxpayers are left holding the bag. It is one thing for society to decide to collect more tax revenues in order to better fund higher education institutions and their students and quite another to provide unplanned and arbitrary subsidies to students selected on the basis of failing to meet their repayment obligations.

Notes

1. Undergraduate students are independent of their parents for financial aid purposes if they are age 24 or older, married, veterans or active military members, foster children, emancipated minors, unaccompanied homeless youth, or if they have dependents of their own.

2. Perkins Loans, a third, much smaller undergraduate loan program, have been funded by a combination of federal and institutional funds. Congress failed to renew this program in 2015.
3. Sandy Baum et al., *Trends in Student Aid 2015* (New York: The College Board, 2015), Table 3.
4. Sandy Baum et al, *Trends in Student Aid 2015*; U.S. Department of Education, "Aid Recipients Summary" Federal Student Aid, 2015, https://studentaid.ed.gov/sa/about/data-center/student/title-iv.
5. Tara Siegel Bernard, "The Many Pitfalls of Private Student Loans," *The New York Times*, September 4, 2015.
6. NCES, National Postsecondary Student Aid Study 2012, Power Stats, http://nces.ed.gov/datalab/.
7. Sandy Baumet al., *Trends in Student Aid 2014* (New York: The College Board, 2014), Figure 16A.
8. Sandy Baum, *A Framework for Thinking About Law School Affordability* (West Chester, PA: The Access Group, 2015).
9. Adam Looney and Constantine Yannelis, "A crisis in student loans? How changes in the characteristics of borrowers and in the institutions they attended contributed to rising loan defaults," *Brookings Papers on Economic Activity*, September 2015.
10. Doug Shapiro et al., *Completing College: A National View of Student Attainment Rates – Fall 2008 Cohort.* Signature Report No. 8 (Herndon, VA: National Student Clearinghouse Research Center, 2014).
11. Sandy Baum et al., *Trends in Student Aid 2015*, Figure 16A.
12. NCES, *Digest of Education Statistics 2014*, (Washington, DC: U.S. Department of Education, 2015), Table 318.40.
13. Sandy Baum et al., *Trends in Student Aid 2015*, Figure 10B.
14. NCES, *Digest of Education Statistics 2014*, Table 303.25.
15. Jennifer Ma et al., *Trends in College Pricing 2015* (New York: The College Board, 2015), Figure 9.
16. Sandy Baum et al., *Trends in Student Aid 2015*, Figure 29A.
17. Jennifer Ma et al., *Trends in College Pricing 2015*, Figure 2.
18. Alan Zarembo, "Generous GI bill isn't keeping today's veterans out of student loan debt," *Los Angeles Times*, October 30, 2015, http://www.latimes.com/nation/la-na-veteran-debt-20151031-story.html.
19. U.S. Department of Education, "National Student Loan Default Rates," Federal Student Aid, 2015, http://www.ifap.ed.gov/eannouncements/attachments/093015AttachOfficialFY20123YRCDRBriefing.pdf.
20. Natasha Burton, "Stressed Over Student Loans? 3 People Share How They're Paying Off Big Debt on Starter Salaries," *Forbes*, August 6, 2015, http://www.forbes.com/sites/learnvest/2015/08/06/stressed-over-student-loans-3-people-share how-theyre-paying-off-big-debt-on-star.

21. U.S. Department of Education, "National Student Loan Default Rates."
22. David Radwin et al., *2011–12 National Postsecondary Student Aid Study (NPSAS:12): Student Financial Aid Estimates for 2011–12*, 2013–165 (Washington, DC: National Center for Education Statistics, 2013).
23. Sandy Baum et al., *Trends in Student Aid 2015*, Figure 14A.

CHAPTER 3

Putting the Stories into Perspective

Abstract Disturbing anecdotes that are real but not representative can capture a lot of attention in the media and cascade into widely accepted panics that are out of proportion to reality. Student debt is just one example of this phenomenon. Some proposed policy responses, such as forgiving and eliminating all student debt, would be very poor strategies even if they were feasible. Increased educational attainment has significant benefits both for society as a whole and for individuals. Although there is significant variation among people with the same level of education, people with college degrees generally earn much more than others. They can reasonably use a portion of their higher incomes to repay debt—as long as there is protection for people who run into unexpected difficulties.

Keywords Student debt • College financing • Debt-free college

If the situation is not as bad as most people think, how has this story taken hold? How can we explain the presence of the very real stories about serious student debt problems? What policy changes might both make those stories more rare and rationalize the sharing of risk and responsibility between borrowers and taxpayers?

S. Baum, *Student Debt*, DOI 10.1057/978-1-137-52738-7_3

Media Sensationalism and the Development of the Common Wisdom

Everyone knows something about student debt. For some people, the knowledge is from their own personal experiences or those of their friends or relatives. For others, it is just from the media. Unfortunately, many anecdotes that provide the grounding for most people's understanding of how students pay for college and how debt affects their lives are not representative. It's not that they aren't true. Most of them may well be accurate accounts. But just as no one writes about people who buy lottery tickets but don't win and planes that land safely don't make headlines, stories about students who borrow reasonable amounts, go to college, graduate, get jobs, and pay back their loans while living normal lives don't capture the attention of journalists.

Generating strong emotional reactions to exaggerated images of problems is not uncommon. An interesting example is the widespread impression that the prominently reported breaches of the computer systems at major retailers and banks have serious repercussions for millions of people and that we should all be quite concerned about the dangers we face from this type of violation. Apparently, the costs are not nearly as high as the frequent reports would suggest. According to a columnist of New York Times' *The Upshot*, only a tiny fraction of the people whose credit information hackers stole at Target or JP Morgan paid any cost at all. Banks and merchants pay most of the costs, and they are finding better ways to stop the breaches from turning into theft. "This relatively sanguine picture of the impact of data breaches is an example of a threat that looks worse than it turns out to be. The sheer size of hackings shocks and startles when the attacks are first reported, but it's rare that journalists check on the actual consequences."[1]

New journalistic efforts to improve the use of statistics bring more such examples to light. Five Thirty Eight Politics investigated the realities behind widespread reports of a new crime wave in spring 2015.[2] *The New York Times* published a prominent article on "Murder Rates Rising Sharply in Many US Cities," opening with the statement that "Cities across the nation are seeing a startling rise in murders after years of declines."[3]

A Five Thirty Eight investigation found that murder rates overall in the 60 largest cities were up by 16% in 2015 relative to 2014. But between 1980 and 2012, the national murder rate fell by more than 50% and year-to-year fluctuations often do not signal trends. There is no obvious reversal of the long-term downward trend.

Reports about disasters create the impression that they are much more common than they actually are, generating disproportionate anxiety. In *The Culture of Fear: Why Americans Are Afraid of the Wrong Things*, Barry Glassner uses the example of "road rage."[4] Googling this term yields a large number of stories with headlines about the frequency of this phenomenon, in addition to frightening individual events. But the American Automobile Association reports that of the 250,000 people killed in auto-related deaths between 1990 and 1997, under 1 in 1000 could be directly attributed to "road rage."[5] Reading the news distorts our impression of the magnitude of the issue.

A more recent example emerges from a Gallup Poll examining Americans' top health care concerns. Ebola, cited by 17% of respondents as the nation's most urgent problem—was the third most commonly cited issue in the survey, despite the fact that there were only four reported cases in the country—hardly on the scale of heart disease, cancer, obesity, and a long list of other possible choices.[6]

The concept of "moral panic" is relevant here. The idea is that fear of some evil threatening the well-being of society spreads among a large number of people. This fear can lead to actions designed to counteract the problem that are disproportionate to the actual threat.[7]

A related concept from the behavioral economics literature is the "availability cascade." An idea, particularly a simple idea that purports to explain a complicated concept or series of events, can take hold in the public discourse. The idea catches on, spreading through social media or other transmission mechanisms. If so many people believe this, maybe it's true. The idea seems reasonable, apparently many people are convinced by it, and actually figuring out the explanations for complex realities is too demanding. This phenomenon can turn media reports of relatively minor events into public panics.

Politicians respond to the public emotion, proposing policy solutions addressing that emotion, rather than considering the most effective strategies for dealing with the problems emerging from solid evidence and analysis. According to Daniel Kahneman in *Thinking, Fast and Slow*, anyone who claims that the danger is overstated is suspected of association with a "heinous cover-up."[8]

Scare stories about student debt are not so different. It is increasingly common to see references to student debt as an unmitigated evil. In a 2014 *Huffington Post* article, the author argues for "civil disobedience on a massive scale" to free millions of former students "trapped in a debtors' prison without walls."[9] The proposed policy solutions are less dramatic than the description of the problem: lowering interest rates on outstanding student loans—an idea advocated by many in Congress and presidential candidates from both parties—and basing loan payments on borrowers' discretionary income—a practice that was legislated by Congress a number of years ago and is becoming increasingly generous from year to year.

Policy Ideas Arising Out of the Panic

Proposals for "debt-free college" and for forgiving all outstanding student debt are exaggerated reactions to a real problem that is much less severe and pervasive than the media would lead us to believe. The "debt-free" idea sounds appealing and it's not so easy to argue that more debt is better than less debt. But the idea that the conversation about student debt has become one where it is radical to argue that it is actually reasonable for people to borrow to invest in their futures is startling—as is the widespread avoidance of the question of the burden on taxpayers if students are not asked to pay any share of the cost of their education.

This focus is problematic because no one actually has a viable plan for how we could make sure that everyone who goes to college could pay their tuition, fees, room, board, and other living expenses with a combination of grant aid and money they have in their pockets (or their parents' pockets) before they have begun their education. It is disturbing because it would involve large public subsidies to some of the more privileged members of society, leaving out many of those facing the largest challenges. It appears to reject the idea that education is an investment that pays off over a lifetime, bringing significant and varied benefits to the individuals who succeed in their studies. And perhaps most worrisome, financing the cost of making college "debt-free" risks leading to underfunding of higher education institutions and the rationing of more limited spaces.

Supporters of the notion of debt-free college can sign a petition online, sponsored by the Progressive Change Campaign Committee, whose goal is to make debt-free college a central issue in the 2016 presidential campaign.[10]

Democrats in Congress have joined the chorus. Twin resolutions in the House and the Senate defining debt-free as "having no debt upon graduation from all public institutions of higher education" have over 70 signatories. The resolution points out that workers with college degrees earn more money than others—which might be interpreted as implying that they have greater than average financial capacity. But without citing evidence, the resolution asserts that student debt constrains career choices, hurts the credit ratings of students, prevents people from fully participating in the economy by purchasing goods and services, and threatens essential milestones of the American dream, including the purchase of a home or car, starting a family, and saving for retirement. The goal is that "all students have access to debt-free higher education, defined to mean having no debt upon graduation from all public institutions of higher education."[11] Chapter 4 addresses the evidence for these claims about the impact of student debt.

The Center for American Progress, "an independent nonpartisan policy institute that is dedicated to improving the lives of all Americans, through bold, progressive ideas, as well as strong leadership and concerted action,"[12] sponsors a website called Higher Ed Not Debt, representing a "multi-year campaign of dozens of organizations dedicated to tackling the crippling and ever-growing issue of student loan debt in America."[13] The title clearly suggests a choice, rather than complementarity between debt and education. Young Invincibles, "a national organization, representing the interests of 18- to 34-year-olds and making sure that our perspective is heard wherever decisions about our collective future are being made,"[14] claims to have a plan that could "unleash the American economy by making graduating from college without debt a reality for millions of young people looking to build a better life."[15] They would give all students a pathway to a debt-free degree, "making debt-free college a reality." Their focus is on students enrolled in public four-year institutions.[16]

Reading carefully makes it clear that most policy advocates and policy makers expressing support for the debt-free concept aren't really talking about doing away with student debt altogether. Most of the proposals on the subject lack detail about what debt-free would really mean, who would be included, and how it would be paid for. One article on the subject quoted Under Secretary of Education Ted Mitchell as saying about debt-free: "We're talking about it and thinking about it. We think that affordability doesn't necessarily end up at zero." And David Bergeron of the supportive Center for American Progress says that we should ensure that everybody has an alternative that is of high quality and free, but "that doesn't necessarily mean completely eliminating loan borrowing for all public university students."[17]

Presidential candidate Martin O'Malley wrote in a *Washington Post* op-ed, "Our ultimate goal must be for every student—most especially low-income and middle-class students—to be able to go to college debt-free."[18]

Demos, which describes itself as "a public policy organization working for an America where we all have an equal say in our democracy and an equal chance in our economy,"[19] released a detailed report in support of debt-free college—a plan that would "ensure the majority of poor-, working- and middle-class students can attend college without incurring debt or financial hardship." Middle-income is defined as 300% of the federal poverty line, or about $73,000 for a family of four.

Even Elizabeth Warren, the most prominent voice in Congress for student debt relief, says, "And while not every college needs to graduate every student debt-free, every kid needs a debt-free option—a strong public university where it's possible to get a great education without taking on loads of debt."[20]

But the idea creeps in even when it is not the preferred direction and observers see it even when it is not there. A headline in the *Washington Post* about a speech by Secretary of Education Arne Duncan in July 2015 announced: "Duncan: Colleges are falling short for millions of students. Debt-free degrees are just part of the solution." According to the Secretary, "There is a path to a higher education system that serves many more students much better. And continuing to make college more accessible and affordable—including more tuition-free and debt-free degrees—is part of that. But it's only part."[21] The speech included emphasis on reducing debt and making college more affordable—but not actually eliminating debt.

Under the headline "Debt-Free Catches On," *Inside Higher Ed* reported that Hillary Clinton, yet to make proposals for improving higher education financing, was on the verge of embracing a debt-free plan.[22] When the candidate did release her plan, it proposed a strategy for debt-free tuition at public colleges and for reducing the burden of debts incurred for living expenses and for private colleges—not for eliminating student debt. Nonetheless, it received quite a bit of praise for being "debt-free." MSNBC announced "Clinton's sweeping new debt-free college plan."[23] According to the *Nation*, "Hillary Clinton Joins Debt-Free Push with a Big Plan."[24] Similarly, Demos advocates announced "The Momentum Builds—Hillary Clinton Releases Debt-Free College Plan."[25]

We should understand both the positive and the negative aspects of making it possible for students—most of whom do not have strong established credit records before they go to college—to borrow to fund their education. In order to fix the problems in our current system, to come as close as possible to eliminating the examples of students for whom student debt becomes a real albatross, and at the same time to ensure that we continue to provide the liquidity that students need to make postsecondary education a reality, we have to be able to talk about debt in a reasoned manner. Perhaps the "debt-free" verbiage is a passing fad. But the problems we face as a society that must both provide opportunity and support a productive labor force are urgent. We can't solve them unless we can focus on realistic and equitable pathways to financing higher education in the USA.

The Positive Impact of Student Loans

The federal student loan system was developed to increase access to postsecondary education. Paying up front for an investment expected to yield positive returns in the future poses liquidity problems. Many individuals with positive expected returns to education cannot borrow on reasonable terms in the private market because they have no collateral and no credit history. The federal government plays an important role in offering credit to students who would not be served well in the private market.

When Lyndon Johnson signed the Higher Education Act in 1965, he had high hopes for the new student aid system, of which federal student loans were an integral part. He argued, "To thousands of young men and women, this act means the path of knowledge is open to all that have the determination to walk it."[26] Access to credit on good terms in combination with need-based grant aid would prevent students from being shut out of higher education because of limited resources.

It is not easy to document the effectiveness of student loans in increasing college access and success. A dollar of grant aid that does not have to be repaid almost certainly has a bigger impact on promoting postsecondary participation than a dollar of loans. But grant dollars are much more costly to the government than loan dollars. And, as discussed throughout this book, the cash flow problems facing students do not, in most cases, signal long-term financial hardship and the need for large public subsidies. So loans make sense.

The availability of credit does appear to provide the boost to college access for which the programs were designed. The strongest evidence comes from other countries, including Chile and South Africa, where the programs appear to significantly reduce financial barriers to enrollment among eligible students.[27] The impact is not necessarily the same in a different culture with a different postsecondary system. But there is quite a bit of suggestive evidence that access to loans increases college opportunities in the USA.[28] The idea is not that loans should replace grants, but that when added to grants as part of a comprehensive student aid system, loans play a positive role, and if designed and administered appropriately, are likely to be a cost-effective means of helping students finance eduction.

Some researchers have suggested that resistance to borrowing, especially among low-income and minority populations, may be causing some students to borrow less than the optimal amount, reducing their chances for earning degrees in a timely manner, or even to give up on college all together.[29]

Society Benefits from Higher Education and so Does the Individual

Public higher education has a long history in the USA, with a broad consensus that an educated populace is important for society as a whole. Historically, states have taken the lead in financing separate systems of public higher education. In 1950, half of all postsecondary students were enrolled in public colleges and universities. Over the next decade, total enrollment grew from 2.3 million to 3.9 million and by 1960, 60% of students were in the public sector. Between 1960 and 1970, total postsecondary enrollment more than doubled and in 1970, 75% of students were enrolled in public institutions. Today, 72% of the nation's 20.2 million postsecondary students attend public colleges and universities.[30]

Most Americans agree that everyone who can benefit should have access to a high-quality, affordable college education and there are both equity and efficiency arguments for public subsidies to colleges and their students. To the extent that education provides the best route for people to improve themselves and their options for financial independence and a rewarding work life, denying access to that pathway to people who do not have the means to pay is unfair. Whether or not one favors redistributing income in the interest of reducing inequality, it is hard to argue that denying individuals the opportunity to gain the knowledge, skills, and modes of thinking they need to succeed is acceptable.

It's not just unfair. It is also inefficient. There is no doubt that some of the benefits of an individual's college education accrue to society as a whole. It is costly to have unproductive members of society, both because they need public support and because they don't add to our overall output. Not educating people who could become more productive with that opportunity is a waste of valuable resources. It shrinks the pie.

In recent years, however, states are providing a smaller share of the necessary resources, leaving students and families with a bigger share. The federal government has taken up some of the slack, increasing the generosity of its support for students. But more and more students and families have strained under the burden of paying costs that before might have been covered by state budgets. As Table 3.1 indicates, the subsidies public college students receive in the form of tuition that is lower than the full cost of education have dwindled over time, with tuition revenues covering an increasing portion of these costs. For example, in 2002–03, students at public doctoral universities benefited from public and institutional resources that allowed 58% of their educational costs to be subsidized, with tuition covering just 42% of the costs. By 2012–13, those roles had been reversed, with tuition revenues covering the 61% of costs that subsidies did not meet.

The sharp decline in per-student state funding for higher education does, to some extent, represent shifting priorities and competing demands on state budgets. But a rapid increase in enrollment has also contributed to the decline in per-student state funding. Over the decade described in Table 3.1, total state appropriations for higher education declined by 9% after adjusting for inflation. But because (full-time equivalent) enrollment increased by 19%, funding per student fell by 24%. With a recovering economy and no enrollment growth over the next two years, both total appropriations and appropriations per student increased by 8% in inflation-adjusted dollars between 2012–13 and 2014–15.

Table 3.1 Covering costs at public colleges and universities over time

		Net Tuition Revenue	Subsidy
Public Doctoral	2002–03	42%	58%
	2007–08	48%	52%
	2012–13	61%	39%
Public Master's	2002–03	41%	59%
	2007–08	47%	53%
	2012–13	61%	39%
Public Bachelor's	2002–03	40%	60%
	2007–08	47%	53%
	2012–13	54%	46%
Public Two-Year	2002–03	26%	74%
	2007–08	29%	71%
	2012–13	39%	61%

Note: Subsidies come primarily from state and local funding

Source: Ma et al., *Trends in College Pricing 2015,* The College Board, Figure 19B

Public Benefits Are Not the Same as Public Goods

It is not uncommon to see the argument that asking students to incur debt to finance their education is tantamount to ignoring the social benefit of higher education. The argument is about whether education is a "private good," with most of the benefits accruing to the students, or a "public good," with large benefits for society as a whole. Sarah Hebel of the *Chronicle of Higher Education* wrote, "Once embraced as a collective good, a public higher education is increasingly viewed—and paid for—as a private one."[31] Catherine Rampell of the *Washington Post* lamented, "Higher Education Went From Being a Public Good to a Private One."[32]

It may be helpful to take a step back to ask whether this is a reasonable dichotomy. Economists have a very useful definition of public goods. Public goods have two characteristics:

1. Non-excludability: It is not possible to exclude non-payers from consuming the good.
2. Non-rivalry in consumption: Allowing additional people to consume the good does not diminish the benefit to others.

National defense is a public good. It is not possible to exclude people who refuse to pay their taxes because they are pacifists from the protections generated by the military. And the fact that such people are included does not diminish the extent to which taxpayers are protected. Another example is mosquito control. If the town sprays, there is no way to keep the bugs swarming around the non-taxpayers. And the reduction in the mosquitoes plaguing me is not affected by the fact that others are also mosquito-free.

In contrast, it is possible to charge admission to concerts in the park and keep non-payers out. This will make a difference to attendees, who might enjoy the event less if it were too crowded. There may be public benefits and the city may be a better place to live even for non-concert-goers, but attendees receive larger benefits than others. Similarly, it is obviously possible to exclude non-payers from higher education. Moreover, congestion is an issue. If too many students are enrolled in an institution, it will be hard to register for classes or class sizes will be larger, diminishing the experience. It costs more to educate a lot of people than it does to educate a few people.

Higher education is *not* a public good by this definition. But that's not to say that society doesn't benefit when people go to college. There are significant "positive externalities" to higher education.

When John goes to college, he gets a high percentage of the benefit. He may well enjoy the activity and the environment. He will learn and have experiences that open doors for the rest of his life. And he will significantly increase his earning potential.

But it's also true that as more people go to college, our society and our economy develop. People with a college education earn more than others, but their higher earnings do not reflect the whole of their contribution. Others who work with them earn higher wages because of the added flexibility, innovation, and productivity of the labor force.[33] People with a college education tend to be more active citizens, with their volunteering and other activities benefiting those around them.[34] There are more new products and services for all of us to enjoy because of the contributions of college graduates.[35]

The most common example of externalities is pollution—a negative externality. If I operate a steel factory, I pay for the labor and other inputs and get the revenues. But I don't pay the full costs—I generate pollution that imposes costs on everyone in the surrounding area. This doesn't make the production of steel a public good, but it does mean it has an impact that extends beyond the direct participants. If I spruce up my yard, my neighbors benefit. They enjoy a positive externality. And if I go to college, my future coworkers benefit because I will be a more productive worker. My community benefits because I will be a better citizen. The economy benefits because I will be self-sufficient.

This is not an either/or question.[36] It is clear that individuals benefit financially and otherwise from postsecondary education. It is also clear that society gets some fraction of the benefits. The positive externality means that public subsidies of higher education are not just equitable, increasing opportunities for those with limited means, but also efficient. The market overproduces goods and services with negative externalities. Steel mill owners don't account for the pollution they generate when making their business decisions. And it underproduces goods and services with positive externalities. Rational individuals will make their college-going decisions based on their own costs and benefits. They won't be willing to bear the cost of improving society.

We should not be debating whether education is a public good or a private good. There are many private benefits, for which individuals should be willing to pay. But there are also public benefits, for which taxpayers as a whole should be willing to pay. The difficult question is what the appropriate breakdown is. How much of the cost of their own education should students be asked to bear and how much should be covered by society?

A national conversation about this appropriate division is vital. But even assuming that the current distribution is skewed too far in the direction of students bearing the burden and taxpayers as a whole not taking enough responsibility, students certainly can and should pay some part of the cost of their education. The alternative to relying on some amount of borrowing among students without parents who are able and willing to shoulder the entire burden is higher taxes. Like debt payments, higher taxes reduce discretionary income, leaving fewer options for personal expenditures.

If students shouldn't have to pay for a portion of their education with their post-college earnings, who *should* pay? One possible response to this question is that we should raise taxes on the wealthy and use the proceeds for pay for college for all. Funding through progressive taxes means that everyone with relatively high incomes pays, whether or not they went to college, whether or not they worked their way through college or their parents paid the whole bill.

But there are a lot of competing demands for those extra tax revenues. Paying for higher education is not the only—or even the most compelling—problem our nation faces. We need better pre-school opportunities and elementary and secondary schools that prepare students from all backgrounds to benefit from higher education and become productive members of society. We need more housing and food security for people who are homeless and hungry. Our roads, bridges, and tunnels are not adequately maintained.

There is a lot of wealth in the USA and the nation certainly has the option of engaging in more collective activity to address these issues. But user fees for college—in the form of tuition—are not unreasonable in this context, especially since people from more affluent backgrounds are most likely to go to college and to stay in college for a longer time. And regardless of their backgrounds, people who participate in higher education tend to end up in the top ranges of the income distribution.

Again, the question is not whether tax revenues should subsidize public higher education. They should. The question is whether it is reasonable to expect individual students to use some of the earnings bump they get from their college education to pay some part of the cost of that education. If so, borrowing for college is reasonable.

Individual Decisions: Are Students Wrong to Incur Debt for College?

The questions of the best way for our society to fund higher education and the appropriate division between public support for students and payments by students who participate are critical issues that will be on the public agenda for years to come. Meanwhile, individuals have to make decisions about whether and where to go to college, whether to borrow to increase their options, and how much they can borrow without digging themselves into a hole.

Despite the deluge of stories and opinion pieces about student debt, it is possible to find an occasional recognition of the positive side of student debt in the popular media: Ben Walsh argued in the *Huffington Post:*

> Still, education is a fantastic way to invest in your own earning potential, and debt is a great way to invest in things that yield predictable returns... Ordinary Americans can get access to loans to buy all sorts of things that fall in value and usefulness shortly after they're bought: cars, clothes, electronics, furniture, appliances. Even homes, which you can take out a mortgage to buy, can rise in value, but their price is volatile, and the thing itself is immobile and requires money to maintain.
>
> A college degree has none of these drawbacks. It's the only type of loan Americans can use to directly invest in their long-term personal economic well-being.
>
> There are lots of bad reasons to go into debt. A college degree is a good reason to borrow money.[37]

We cannot lose track of this argument and we should find ways to communicate it more widely. The operative question for students making decisions today about where, when, and what to study is how to make the best decisions given the current tuition and financial aid systems. Is the amount of debt required unmanageable? Does it make the investment in education a bad one with a negative expected return? Or is it a good investment that will leave the borrower better off than if he or she had not followed that path?

Even if it would be more equitable or more efficient for taxpayers to shoulder more of the burden of financing postsecondary education and students to shoulder less of the burden, most potential students will be better off incurring the necessary debt and getting an education than they would be skipping the investment.

It is helpful to compare college to other activities frequently financed through borrowing. It is reasonable to rely on credit for home purchases for a few reasons. One is that you will live in the house for many years, so it is logical to pay over time for the services of the home. This argument also applies to consumer durables. Most people rely on loans to purchase cars. The idea is that they can pay off the loan over the years that they are driving the car, rather than paying for it all at once.

People also take out loans to start new businesses. If they waited to save up all the money required to invest in the business, they would probably never get to the starting line. The accepted approach is to make a good business plan and evaluate the probable returns to the investment. If the plan works out as anticipated, the returns will be high enough to make the loan payments and still have funds left over both to live and to reinvest in the company.

Borrowing for college has a similar logic. Higher education is an investment that pays off over time. College graduates have much higher earnings, on average, than similar people who do not go to college. The earnings premium is large enough to make loan payments and still live at a higher standard of living than would have been possible without the investment in education.

So borrowing for college is not like borrowing for a vacation. However, education loans carry some risks for both borrowers and lenders that distinguish them from other types of "good" debt. A key issue is that the investment is in *human* capital. If you buy a house and then realize that the loans are too expensive, in most markets you can sell the house and get at least a high percentage of your money back.

Lenders are willing to make loans for houses and for small businesses even though there is some risk involved. If a homeowner fails to pay his mortgage or a car purchaser fails to make loan payments, the lender can repossess the house or the car. If a small business fails to generate the anticipated returns, there may be some physical assets that could be sold to generate cash.

But a college education cannot be sold or repossessed. This creates added risk for both the borrower and the lender. And the returns are uncertain. The fact that returns are high on average and for most people does not mean that higher education pays off well for everyone.

Going to College Leads to Higher Earnings

Comparing the earnings of typical college graduates to the earnings of typical high school graduates does not tell an individual how much more he or she will earn if she goes to college. One issue is that people who go to college are different in systematic ways from people who do not. People who earn bachelor's degrees are more likely than people with no college education to have characteristics that would serve them well in the labor market even if they did not continue their education after high school. But careful studies suggest that the average earnings premium is quite close to estimates of how much college actually causes earnings to increase.[38]

In 2014, when median earnings for 35- to 44-year-old high school graduates were $31,300, the median for bachelor's degree holders was $56,100. Table 3.2 includes information on other levels of education and other age groups. The data reveal that, for example, median earnings for 25- to 34-year-old bachelor's degree recipients exceed median earnings for high school graduates in that age group by almost $18,000 a year—almost $1500 a month. It would require debt of over $70,000 to generate monthly payments equal to half that earnings premium with 5% interest and a ten-year repayment period.

There is considerable variation in post-college earnings and of course uncertainty in predicting earnings. Nonetheless, anticipated earnings are central to most decisions to enroll in postsecondary education and ignoring them makes any analysis of affordability incomplete. In a recent attempt to outline benchmarks for how much students can afford to pay for college, Lumina Foundation left borrowing out of the basic calculation, explaining: "This benchmark is constructed with a reasonable saving rate so that students, in an ideal world, do not have to borrow for their postsecondary education."[39] Again, the general sense of student debt as a serious general problem can lead to inadequate attention to the lifetime earnings of students, which should logically factor into the value of their education and the optimal

Table 3.2 Median earnings by education level, 2014

Median Earnings 2014	Ages 25–34	Ages 35–44	Ages 45–54
High School	$26,500	$31,300	$33,600
Some College No Degree	$26,800	$36,100	$39,500
Associate Degree	$30,900	$40,300	$42,100
Bachelor's Degree	$44,200	$56,100	$59,800
Bachelor's Degree or Higher	$47,300	$61,400	$65,400
Monthly Earnings Premium			
High School	$0	$0	$0
Some College No Degree	<$100	$400	$500
Associate Degree	$400	$800	$700
Bachelor's Degree	$1,500	$2,100	$2,200
Bachelor's Degree or Higher	$1,700	$2,500	$2,700

Source: US Census Bureau (2015), *Current Population Survey: Income,* Table PINC-03.

Everyone Doesn't Have the Same Great Outcome

College is supposed to be a solution to financial problems. Sacrifice for a few years, get a college degree, and you will reap significant financial (and nonfinancial) benefits throughout your life. This is an accurate story. But it is accurate on average and for most people most of the time. Not every college education pays off for every individual. During weak economic times, there are more people who struggle even with a college degree.

Significant earnings premiums for postsecondary education do not guarantee that everyone who goes to college will experience the financial benefits. In 2014, 20% of four-year college graduates earned less than the median for high school graduates and 17% of high school graduates earned more than the median for college graduates.[40] Finding individuals with college degrees whose earnings match those of typical high school graduates is not inconsistent with the important reality that higher education pays off well for most students—both financially and otherwise. The payoff is more than adequate to support the repayment of the debt most students incur.

If the justification for borrowing to pay for college lies with the financial returns over time, but there is variation in the returns, it is logical to ask how well we can predict the circumstances under which the investment will pay off well.

How much debt is reasonable? The answer to this question depends on the profile of post-college earnings. It is easy to tell an individual who expects to work at the minimum wage for his entire life, no matter what level of education he attains, that he should refrain from borrowing because he will not be able to support a reasonable lifestyle, much less make student loan payments. (The aspiring organic farmer in Chap. 1 should not have borrowed if he had any idea in advance about his preferred lifestyle.) A young person virtually assured a management position in her father's successful real estate firm may not need to borrow, but could reasonably expect to support fairly high debt payments if she did. Most people fall between these two extremes and have quite a bit of uncertainty about where they will end up.

But some data on the post-college earnings of students attending different colleges and universities and majoring in different areas are available. The federal government's new College Scorecard provides rough data on the earnings of students who received federal financial aid—including federal loans.[41] The Bureau of Labor Statistics reports earnings across occupations[42] and researchers have published information about earnings differentials by major and program of study.[43]

It is also possible to make some judgment calls. A student who borrows $100,000 at a 5% interest rate and expects to pay the debt off over ten years will have payments of $1060 per month, or almost $13,000 per year. For an undergraduate aspiring to earn a bachelor's degree in social work and develop a career as a school social worker, where average earnings are about $46,000 a year,[44] this is not likely to be a good plan. He should enroll in a less expensive institution, live at a lower standard of living while in school, or work more hours while in school (but not so many hours as to interfere with timely graduation) in order to avoid this level of debt—which is far above average for bachelor's degree recipients. On the other hand, these debt payments would be quite reasonable for a dentist, entering a profession with average earnings of over $170,000 per year.

Some of the concerns about holding borrowers responsible for their debts center on the young age at which many people sign for these obligations. There is no doubt that most 18-year-olds have virtually no experience with personal finance and have difficulty evaluating the promise they are making to repay their loans far in the future.[45]

In some countries, national service and/or military duty lead to postponement of college entry for most people. But short of a dramatic change in our social norms, American high school graduates will continue to go straight to college in large numbers. Many of them will be unable to pursue their ambitions without the liquidity provided by student loans. Requiring an older, financially secure co-signer for these loans would limit access for the very people about whom we are most concerned.

Moreover, 18 is the age of majority for most purposes and in most states.[46] While we don't allow 18-year-olds to buy beer, we do send them off to war, allow them to marry without parental consent, and sentence them as adults for criminal acts. It's hard to argue that we should not hold them responsible for repaying their student loans.

Perhaps more important, teenage borrowing is a small part of the problem. The locus of the student debt problem is not traditional-age students enrolling in four-year colleges shortly after graduating from high school. Rather, it is older students, most of whom enroll in community colleges or for-profit institutions.

As discussed earlier, it is students who don't complete credentials and who are enrolled outside the traditional four-year institutions who are most likely to default on their loans. And defaulters have lower average balances than those who repay their debts. Defaulters also come disproportionately from disadvantaged backgrounds and have weak labor market outcomes.[47]

Just as we have to reimagine what college students look like to better structure the student aid system and the way credentials are designed, recognizing that the student debt problem is most acute among the students who don't fit the picture of kids going off to live in dormitories for four years is an important step in designing targeted and constructive policy solutions.

Some decisions about borrowing quite predictably lead to problems. The solution is not to make it easy for anyone interested in going to college to borrow as much as they want and then deal with the resulting unmanageable debt burdens. Rather, we should design loan programs and, perhaps most important, guidance for enrolling students, to minimize the frequency of these untenable outcomes. The final chapter of this book discusses potential approaches to mitigating this problem.

Notes

1. Nathaniel Popper, "Stolen Consumer Data is a Smaller Problem Than it Seems," *The New York Times,* The Upshot, August 2, 2015, http://www.nytimes.com/2015/08/02/business/stolen-consumer-data-is-a-smaller-problem-than-it-seems.html?_r=0&abt=0002&abg=1.
2. Carl Bialik, "Scare Headlines Exaggerated the U.S. Crime Wave," *Five Thirty-Eight Politics,* September 11, 2015, http://fivethirtyeight.com/features/scare-headlines-exaggerated-the-u-s-crime-wave/.
3. Monica Davey and Rich Smith, "Murder Rates Rising Sharply in Many U.S. Cities," *The New York Times,* August 31, 2015, http://www.nytimes.com/2015/09/01/us/murder-rates-rising-sharply-in-many-us-cities.html.
4. Barry Glassner, *The Culture of Fear: Why Americans Are Afraid of the Wrong Things* (New York: Basic Books, 1999).
5. AAA Foundation for Traffic Safety. "'Road Rage' On the Rise," accessed September 20, 2015, https://www.aaafoundation.org/sites/default/files/roadragePR.pdf.
6. Lydia Saad, "Ebola Ranks Among Americans' Top Three Health Concerns," *Gallup*, November 17, 2–14, http://www.gallup.com/poll/179429/ebola-ranks-among-americans-top-three-healthcare-concerns.aspx.
7. Wikipedia, "Moral Panic," accessed 11/10/2015, https://en.wikipedia.org/wiki/Moral_panic.
8. Daniel Kahneman, *Thinking, Fast and Slow* (New York: Farrar, Straus and Giroux, 2011).

9. Bill Zimmerman, "How to Save the Victims of the Student Loan Crisis," *Huffington Post*, April 14, 2014, http://www.huffingtonpost.com/bill-zimmerman/how-to-save-the-victims-o_b_4776528.html.
10. Progressive Change Campaign Committee, "Sign the Petition for Debt-Free College," accessed 10/15/2015, http://act.boldprogressives.org/survey/survey_freecollege/#ProgressiveBudget.
11. U.S. House of Representatives, "H.Res.214," accessed November 2, 2015, http://www.gpo.gov/fdsys/pkg/BILLS-114hres214ih/pdf/BILLS-114hres214ih.pdf.
12. Center for American Progress, "About the Center for American Progress," accessed November 2, 2015, https://www.americanprogress.org/about/mission/.
13. Higher Ed Not Debt, accessed November 2, 2015, http://higherednot-debt.org/.
14. Young Invincibles, accessed November 2, 2015, http://younginvincibles.org/about/.
15. Young Invincibles, "A Higher Education Promise for the 21st Century," June 2015, http://younginvincibles.org/wp-content/uploads/2015/06/YI-Higher-Ed-Agenda.pdf.
16. Elsewhere, Young Invincibles argue that student loans increase access to college and that a well-designed system of income-driven repayment is appropriate public policy. See Jen Mishory and Rory O'Sullivan, *The Student Perspective on Federal Financial Aid Reform*, (Washington, DC: Young Invincibles, 2012).
17. Michael Stratford, "Debt-Free and (Mostly) Detail-Free," June 19, 2015, https://www.insidehighered.com/news/2015/06/19/debt-free-movement-colleges-see-challenges-and-opportunities-few-details.
18. Martin O'Malley, "Federal Solutions to Our Student Loan Problem," April23,2015,https://www.washingtonpost.com/opinions/federal-solutions-to-our-student-loan-problem/2.
19. Demos, "About Demos," accessed November 2, 2015, http://www.demos.org/about-demos.
20. Elizabeth Warren, "The Affordability Crisis: Rescuing the Dream of College Education for the Working class and Poor," Shanker Institute and the American Federation of Teachers, accessed November 10, 2015, http://www.warren.senate.gov/files/documents/ShankerInstitute-AFTEducationSpeech.pdf.
21. Nick Anderson, "Duncan: Colleges are falling short for millions of students. Debt-free degrees are just part of the solution," *Washington Post*, July 27, 2015, http://www.washingtonpost.com/news/grade-point/wp/2015/07/27/duncan-colleges-are-falling-short-for-millions-of-students-debt-free-degrees-are-just-part-of-the-solution/.

22. Michael Stratford, "Debt-Free Catches On," *Inside Higher Ed*, May 11, 2015, https://www.insidehighered.com/news/2015/05/11/wpush-liberals-debt-free-college-gains-traction-2016-democratic-campaign.
23. Adam Seitz-Wald, "Clinton's sweeping new debt-free college plan," *MSNBC*,August10,2015,http://www.msnbc.com/msnbc/clintons-sweeping-new-debt-free-college-plan.
24. George Zornick, "Hillary Clinton Joins Debt-Free College Push With a Big Plan," *The Nation*, August 11, 2015, http://www.thenation.com/article/hillary-clinton-joins-debt-free-college-push-with-a-big-plan/.
25. Tamara Draut, "The Momentum Builds—Hillary Clinton Releases Debt-Free College Plan," *Demos*, August 10, 2015, http://www.demos.org/policyshop.
26. Lyndon Johnson, "Remarks on Signing the Higher Education Act of 1965," Texas State University, accessed October 15, 2015, http://www.txstate.edu/commonexperience/pastsitearchives/2008-2009/lbjresources/higheredact.html.
27. Alex Solis, "Credit access and college enrollment," Paper presented at the 2015 meeting of the American Economic Association, Boston, MA, https://www.aeaweb.org/aea/2015conference/program/retrieve.php?pdfid=862; Marc Guragand, Adrien Lorenceau, and Thomas Mélonio, "Student loans: Liquidity constraint and higher education in South Africa," Agence Française de Développement Working Paper No. 117. 2011.
28. Donald Heller, "The impact of loans on student access," in *The effectiveness of student aid policies: What the research tells us*, ed. Sandy Baum, Michael McPherson, and Patricia Steele (New York: The College Board, 2008); Susan Dynarski, "Loans, Liquidity and Schooling Decisions," Harvard University, 2005; Mark Wiederspan, "Denying loan access: The student-level consequences when community colleges opt out of the Stafford loan Program," CAPSEE, July 2015; Erin Dunlop, "What do Stafford loans actually buy you? The effect of Stafford loan access on community college students," CALDER Working Paper No. 94 (Washington, DC: National Center for Analysis of Longitudinal Data in Education Research, 2013).
29. Christopher Avery and Sarah Turner, "Too College Students Borrow Too Much—Or Not Enough?" *Journal of Economic Perspectives*, 26 (1: 2012): 165–192; Philip Oreopoulos and Uros Petronijevic, "Making College Worth It: A Review of the Returns to Higher Education," *The Future of Children*, 23:1(2013): 41–64.
30. NCES, *Digest of Education Statistics 2014* (Washington, DC: U.S. Department of Education, 2015), Table 303.10.
31. Sara Hebel, "From Public Good to Private Good: How Higher Education Got to a Tipping Point." *The Chronicle of Higher Education*, March 3, 2014, http://chronicle.com/article/From-Public-Good-to-Private/145061.
32. Catherine Rampell, "Higher education went from being a public good to a private one," *Washington Post*, May 22, 2014, http://www.washington-

post.com/opinions/catherine-rampell-higher-education-went-from-being-a-public-good-to-a-private-one/2014/05/22/50263a16-e1bd-11e3-9743-bb9b59cde7b9_story.html.

33. Enrico Moretti, "Estimating the social return to higher education: Evidence from longitudinal and repeated cross-sectional data," *Journal of Econometrics,* 12(2004):175–212.
34. Sandy Baum, Jennifer Ma, and Kathleen Payea, *Education Pays: The Benefits of Higher Education for Individuals and Society* (New York: The College Board, 2013).
35. Sandy Baum and Michael McPherson, "Is Education a Public Good or a Private Good?", *Chronicle of Higher Education,* January 18, 2013, http://chronicle.com/blogs/innovations/is-education-a-public-good-or-a-private-good/28329.
36. George Leef, "College Education is not a Public Good." National Association of Scholars, June 28, 2012,http://www.nas.org/articles/college_education_is_not_a_public_good. Leef argues that individuals should pay for their own education out of their future earnings without public subsidy.
37. Ben Walsh, "The One Argument in Favor of Student Loans," *Huffington Post,* October 2, 2014, http://www.huffingtonpost.com/2014/10/02/student-loan-benefits_n_5916512.html.
38. David Card, "Estimating the Return to Schooling: Progress on Some Persistent Econometric Problems," *Econometrica,* 69 (5, 2001): 1127–1160; Michael Hout, "Social and Economic Returns to Higher Education in the United States," *American Review of Sociology,* 38 (2012):379–400; Clive Belfield and Thomas Bailey, "The Benefits of Attending Community College: A Review of the Evidence," *Community College Review,* 39 (2014): 46–68; Pedro Carniero, James Heckman, and Edward Vytlacil, "Estimating Marginal Returns to Education," *American Economic Review,* 101(6: 2011): 2754–2781.
39. Lumina Foundation, *A Benchmark for Making College Affordable: The Rule of 10* (Indianapolis: Lumina Foundation, 2015), https://www.luminafoundation.org/files/resources/affordability-benchmark-1.pdf.
40. U.S. Census Bureau, Current Population Survey, 2015 Annual Social and Economic Supplement, PINC-03, https://www.census.gov/hhes/www/cpstables/032015/perinc/toc.htm.
41. U.S. Department of Education, "College Scorecard," accessed November 15, 2015, https://collegescorecard.ed.gov/.
42. Bureau of Labor Statistics, "Overview of U.S. Wage Data by Area and Occupation," accessed November 2, 2015, http://www.bls.gov/bls/blswage.htm.
43. Anthony Carnevale, Ben Cheah, and Andrew Hanson, *The Economic Value of College Majors,* (Washington, DC: Georgetown University Center on Education and the Workforce, 2015); Mark Schneider, "Higher Education Pays: But A Lot More for Some Graduates Than for Others," *American*

Institutes for Research, September 3, 2013, http://www.air.org/resource/higher-education-pays-lot-more-some-graduates-others.
44. Bureau of Labor Statistics, "May 2014 National Occupational Employment and Wage Estimates, United States," accessed November 20, 2015, http://www.bls.gov/oes/current/oes_nat.htm#23-0000.
45. Rachel Dwyer, Laura McCloud, and Randy Hodson, "Youth debt, mastery, and self-esteem: Class-stratified effects of indebtedness on self-concept," *Social Science Research*, 40 (3:2011): 727–741, found that both education debt and credit card debt increase the sense of mastery and self-esteem amount young adults. They argue that borrowers tend to view the debt as an investment in the future.
46. USLegal.com, "Age of Majority," accessed November 5, 2015, http://minors.uslegal.com/age-of-majority/.
47. Adam Looney and Constantine Yannelis, "A crisis in student loans? How changes in the characteristics of borrowers and in the institutions they attended contributed to rising loan defaults," *Brookings Papers on Economic Activity*, September 2015.

CHAPTER 4

The Evidence About the Impact of Student Debt

Abstract Many assertions about the impact of student debt are grounded in weak evidence and problematic reasoning. It is difficult to sort out cause and effect, as opposed to similar trends, in much of the analysis of the relationship between student debt and asset formation, entrepreneurial activity, and home purchases. Few discussions of student debt clarify the alternatives—if people didn't borrow for college would they manage to get the same education? If students didn't borrow, who would pay and what would be the impact of higher taxes or reduced spending in other areas? Moreover, surveys of what people believe to be true are too often confused with evidence about what is actually true.

Keywords Student debt • College financing • Student debt and home ownership • Student debt and business formation

To understand how student debt affects individuals and how the amount borrowed to pay for education affects society and the economy as a whole, we need a counterfactual—an alternative scenario to use as a comparison. The alternative is definitely not everyone having the same level of education without anyone paying for it. If students don't borrow, either they will have to pay in another way or someone else will have to pay.

S. Baum, *Student Debt*, DOI 10.1057/978-1-137-52738-7_4

The Great Recession

The Great Recession caused many problems for many people. The unemployment rate rose from 4.6% in January 2007 to 9.8% in January 2010.[1] The annual number of home foreclosures rose by 73% from 2.2 million in 2007 to 3.8 million in 2010.[2] State tax revenues declined and funding for public higher education suffered. More people enrolled in college because they couldn't find good jobs. Published tuition increased sharply. More people took out student loans. Those who graduated (or left school without a degree) had trouble finding good jobs—although they did much better than those without a college education. It is not surprising that the story of a student debt "crisis" has reached such a crescendo in the wake of a terrible recession.

But now that the economy is recovering, the unemployment rate has fallen back to a more usual level, college enrollments are declining somewhat as people find better labor market opportunities, fewer students are borrowing and those who borrow are borrowing a little less—it is time to take a step back and examine the real problems associated with student debt.

Too many students who borrow for postsecondary education end up with very real and avoidable problems. But generalizing from their situations to conclude that borrowing for college is a mistake for individuals, an enormous inequity, and a practice that stifles social mobility is an error that could exacerbate all of the problems generating concern. Chapter 3 cited claims that college debt was to blame for delayed homeownership, delayed marriage, and other important steps in life. This chapter examines the evidence supporting such claims.

Focusing on Total Outstanding Student Debt

Discussions of student debt used to focus on the amount borrowed by individual students, but the aggregate amount of outstanding education debt has become the metric of choice since it passed the $1 trillion dollar mark. There is no doubt that outstanding debt has grown rapidly. That trend is positively correlated with everything else that has gone up over the past decade. But we need more to assert that student loan debt is the primary *cause* of a decline in home purchases by young people across the nation or that it is hobbling a generation.

It is not always easy to distinguish between causation and correlation in judging evidence. Some correlations are simply random. For example, the amount of outstanding student debt is positively correlated with college tuition and with the number of people enrolling in college, but also with the number of people in the USA over the age of 65, and the percentage of Americans who own smartphones. Similarly, the amount of student debt is negatively correlated with the portion of public higher education costs covered by state appropriations, but also with the percentage of the population opposing same-sex marriage and the percentage of people without access to the Internet, and of greater interest, with the percentage of all household income in the USA received by those at the very top of the income distribution.

In some cases, a third factor may be the cause of two other phenomena, which are then correlated. In the case of student debt, does student debt cause the gap in net worth between young adults who borrowed for college and those who did not, or do affluent parents allow some individuals to be both able to graduate from college debt-free and able to accumulate assets quickly?

Causation is not simple. It is rare that one factor alone causes a significant result. Smoking "causes" lung cancer, but not every smoker gets lung cancer and some non-smokers do. It might be better to say that smoking promotes or increases the probability of lung cancer.

If you read a study showing that people who exercise regularly have more positive attitudes, does this mean that if you start exercising your attitude will improve? Maybe. But perhaps people with positive attitudes are more likely to engage in regular exercise. This question of cause and effect is critical for understanding student debt. Large numbers of students who do not complete their courses of study default on their student loans. If we could just get them through their programs, would they then repay their loans? Maybe—there is good reason to expect that they would have higher incomes. But we also know that people who do not complete their programs are more likely to enroll in lower-quality institutions and programs, to have weak academic preparation, to face more personal barriers like work and family obligations or health or financial problems, and possibly to be less committed to their educational pathways.

Awarding them credentials without addressing those problems might well have minimal impact on their earnings, their fundamental life circumstances, or their attitudes toward their debt. Other factors may cause the lack of success both in school and in loan repayment.

What Is the Right Comparison?

To what should we compare the current debt patterns?

From the perspective of an individual student, the choice is frequently to borrow money to go to college; to borrow less money and go to a less desirable institution or work more while enrolled in college part time, increasing the time to degree; or not to enroll in college at all to avoid borrowing.

It is not very constructive to compare students' well-being with a college degree and $25,000 in student debt to what their lives would be like with the same degree and no debt. The latter would be better for them. They would have more discretionary income. They could save more, consume more, and even make the choice to take more satisfying jobs that pay less. With the possible exception of cases where young people are determined to declare their independence from their parents, it is probably not possible to find a student who turned down a free ride in favor of paying her own way at that same institution.

So to analyze the impact of student debt on individuals, we have to ask where they would be if they had not borrowed. Would they have graduated a year or two later and given up the earnings that would have come with entering the job market sooner with a college degree? Would they have left school without degrees because of the financial pressures making it impossible to make ends meet? Would they have gone straight into the labor market after high school instead of going to college? Or would they have managed to get the same education with the same outcomes and have the same jobs now, but no debt payments?

It's a little different to think about the alternative for society as a whole. A number of circumstances could reduce student borrowing:

- Fewer students enroll in college.
- Students stay in college for shorter periods of time.
- Students attend colleges with lower net prices.
- Colleges educate students at lower cost without a reduction in quality.
- Colleges provide lower-quality education at lower cost.
- Enrollment is limited to students who can afford to pay on their own or with support from their families.
- Private donors voluntarily cover more of the cost of education for students.
- More of the cost of education is covered by state and/or federal governments, either through higher taxes or through reduced spending in other areas.

Most people who are concerned about student debt and worried about its impact on the lives of students are probably most interested in some combination of reduced costs while maintaining access and quality, and more coverage of cost through tax revenues rather than tuition.

Accurately analyzing the impact of this scenario is not easy. At a minimum, it requires including accounting for higher tax rates and/or reductions in other government expenditures. Assuming the tax increase would be on higher earners, college-educated individuals would to some extent trade loan payments for higher tax bills. Unfortunately, studies of the impact of student debt rarely, if ever, examine the impact of alternative means of financing education.

It's Not Easy to Study the Impact of Student Debt

The best way to study cause and effect is through experiments. New drugs are frequently tested by randomly dividing people into two groups and giving members of one group the drug while the other group receives a placebo. If the people in the two groups are essentially indistinguishable, with the drug the only difference, better outcomes for the treated groups provide evidence that the drug caused those better outcomes. It is possible to randomly assign students either to receive an extra $10,000 in gift aid or not to receive that funding, and researchers have conducted experiments like this.[3] Not surprisingly, the students receiving the money are usually better off in some way, although the results in terms of educational outcomes of enrolled students are usually not as dramatic as we might hope.

Some studies are based on natural experiments. They look at how things changed when a program was suddenly implemented or discontinued, and compare the change to a similar environment that was not affected. Studies of programs such as state merit scholarships in Georgia, generous tuition assistance in Washington, DC, Social Security survivor benefits, and guaranteed tuition payments for residents of a specific city suggest that these programs have had a significant impact on college enrollment.[4]

Unfortunately, studying the impact of providing extra funding in the form of loans rather than grants has proven to be a much more challenging research endeavor. It is pretty clear that giving people money is better for them than not giving them money, that getting a grant is better for an individual than getting a loan—and that money alone does not ensure good outcomes.

But asking whether having more money is better than having less money is not sufficient for understanding the impact of student loans. For individual students, the operative question is whether they would have been better off not taking the loans and living with the alternatives—which would involve some other cost. For society as a whole, the question is an even more complicated one, involving comparisons of the impact of different uses of resources.

Studies of the Impact of Student Debt

Journalists frequently state as a given that student debt is having significant negative effects on the economy and on the lives of borrowers. These are usually general statements, not focusing on the minority of borrowers for whom life is almost certainly worse than it would have been if they had never borrowed—and never gone to school. As we have seen, there is wide variation in levels of debt, in the type of education funded with that debt, in the characteristics of the students borrowing, and in both their educational and their labor market outcomes. It seems quite clear that student debt has generated serious harm to some individuals. But that is not the same thing as either student debt causing major problems across the economy or student debt negatively affecting the lives of all or most borrowers.

Assertions of negative effects are certainly not made up out of thin air, but they are also not well grounded in evidence. A number of scholars are asking questions about the impact of student debt and trying to develop sound tests to answer these questions. Unfortunately, limited data and methodological difficulties make it challenging to get reliable answers. In particular, the studies rarely, if ever, ask what the trade-offs would be if resources were transferred to students from others.

Does Student Debt Stop People from Accumulating Wealth?

It would be surprising if individuals with similar levels of education and similar incomes who are repaying student loans were able to save and accumulate assets at the same rate as those without these obligations. A \$300 a month loan payment may be quite manageable, but without it, an individual could either increase his or her consumption or save more. It would also be surprising if people whose parents paid for college, relieving them of the burden of having to borrow, did not receive greater post-college support than their peers from less affluent backgrounds.

What makes it possible for some students to graduate without debt while their classmates are forced to borrow? In most cases, parental resources limit the need for students to borrow. Among 2011–12 bachelor's degree recipients, 45% of those from the highest family income quartile graduated without debt, compared to just 21% of those from the lower half of the income distribution.[5] But the children of affluent parents enjoy much more than just college without debt. Their parents may support them the summer after graduation so they can take an unpaid internship that will open professional doors. Their parents may pay the security deposit when they rent an apartment. And their parents may provide at least part of the down payment for a house. In other words, the absence of student debt and the accumulation of assets may both be the result of parental support.

Although it is clear that much of the asset accumulation of young people is a function of the financial circumstances and generosity of their parents, a Pew Research Center study suggests that student debt has led to differences in wealth accumulation that far exceed typical debt levels. Pew found that based on the Survey of Consumer Finances, college-educated adults without any student debt obligations have about seven times the typical net worth ($64,700) of households with similar characteristics headed by a young, college-educated adult with student debt ($8700). The author acknowledges that other factors are also at work, but the clear implication is that it is student debt that is putting young people's economic well-being in jeopardy. Interestingly, the study points out that student debtors also tend to have more of other kinds of debt, such as credit card and auto loans—and mortgage debt.[6] Is this because student debt leaves them unable to purchase necessities? Is it because the student debt is a symptom of a lack of underlying resources that also makes buying a car more difficult? Given the association with mortgage debt, is it related to relative trends in the value of houses and other assets or to choices about paying down student debt?

Does Student Debt Stop People from Starting Businesses?

A 2015 *Wall Street Journal* (*WSJ*) headline proclaimed: "Want to be an entrepreneur? Beware of student debt." The article began by asserting that "Student loans and small businesses don't mix."[7] The story was based on one study that, largely because of constraints on the data available, looked at net business formations at the county level and at the percentage of consumer debt in the county that was in the form of student debt. As the authors note, the absence of individual level data is a real problem.

The study found that there was a lower net increase in the number of businesses with one to four employees in counties where student loan debt increased relative to other forms of consumer debt. The result did not hold for larger businesses that, the authors assert, are less dependent on personal access to credit for the entrepreneurs.[8] In this study, it is not the amount of student debt, but student debt as a percentage of total consumer debt that is at issue. And it is not the number of businesses that are started, but the net growth in small businesses. A county with a lot of small business failures would have a low rate of growth even if its rate of start-ups was average, but the authors cannot capture this distinction. The authors hypothesize that the other forms of consumer debt may be used to finance the businesses. If this is the case then when people start businesses, the ratio of student debt to other debt declines because credit card debt and other personal debt increase to fund the business. But then it doesn't make much sense to say that this decline in the ratio of student debt caused the increase in business formation.

A recent Gallup-Purdue public opinion poll found that "More than a third of recent graduates with student loans (36 percent) say they have delayed buying a home—a significant concern given the US economy's connection to the country's housing market. One-third (33 percent) say they have postponed buying a car. Also important from an economic perspective, 19 percent of recent graduates who took out student loans—and 25 percent of those with loans totaling over $25,000—say the debt has forced them to delay starting their own business."[9]

The survey asks about perceptions. It makes no attempt to collect actual evidence on college graduates taking steps toward starting new businesses. Yet a blog post from Gallup reporting on the survey is headlined "Student Loan Debt: Major Barrier to Entrepreneurship."[10] It's not hard to see how an interesting observation about the responses college graduates give to a survey turns into a widespread belief that there is evidence of cause and effect, when no such evidence actually exists.

According to the *WSJ*, reporting on the survey, "The conclusion, the researchers believe, is that prospective entrepreneurs are so burdened with student debt that they simply can't take on any more debt to start a business."[11]

But, "That said, the report comes with a caveat: While the paper does identify a correlation between higher student debt and lower small-business formation, the authors can't prove their theory that heavy debt burdens can keep people from pursuing entrepreneurship." They do not claim to have found a causal link. In other words, if you read to the end of the *WSJ* article, you will see that the assertion at the beginning, that we now know that student debt causes small business formation to decline, does not really emerge from the study. As one of the authors is quoted as pointing out, it is possible that people with a lot of student debt move to areas with large employers, making those areas look more debt-burdened. It is, of course, also possible that people without student debt have parents who have paid for college and can now seed business start-ups.

Raising further doubts about causation, an article in *Entrepreneurship* argues that the fraction of young people who own their own companies has been declining for nearly 25 years and we should look for explanations beyond student debt. Young people likely have changing priorities unrelated to student debt.[12]

Overall, there is no solid evidence about student debt being a significant cause of declining entrepreneurship among young people.[13] But in the rush to find a culprit for most of the problems facing our society today, student debt is a good target.

Does Student Debt Stop People from Buying Houses?

Probably the most commonly cited concern relates to whether student debt prevents young people from being able to buy houses. This is usually a broad question about student debt overall and housing purchases overall, not about particular subsets of individuals. It seems quite logical that people would either postpone the purchase of a home or buy a cheaper house than they would if they had the same income but no education debt. But we have to know both what individuals' circumstances would actually be if they had not borrowed and how their education may have affected them beyond the debt they incurred. Perhaps education makes people more aware of the recent financial crisis and the risks involved in home ownership. Perhaps it leads them to postpone marriage, childbearing, and the concomitant desire to buy a house.

If the class of 2015 graduated from college debt-free, they would almost certainly be a bigger presence in the housing market over the next decade than they will in fact be, given their debt. However, if lower education debt burdens emerged from more generous public funding of education, higher tax payments would probably also be part of the scenario, partially counteracting the increases in disposable income among former students. In other words, the question is not what home purchases would look like if there were more money all around, but what they would look like if there were transfers to students from someone else.

If the absence of debt meant lower levels of educational attainment, this group of students would have lower incomes and diminished wherewithal to finance home purchases. If their parents had paid higher taxes to better fund the state governments that have cut back on their financing of public higher education, they might not have been able to help as much with down payments for their children's houses.

The Federal Reserve Bank of New York, which bases its analyses of student debt on a nationally representative sample of people with credit reports,[14] is the source of much of the available information on outstanding student loan balances.[15] Researchers there have attempted to document the relationship between home purchases and student debt. One study compared the proportion of 30-year-olds with home-secured debt among those with and without a history of student loans. They found that between 2003 and 2011, those who had borrowed for college were more likely to have mortgages than those who had not, but that the relationship reversed in 2011 as home ownership rates fell more for those who had borrowed for college than for those who had not.[16] The authors do not claim that increases in student loan debt actually caused this change. It is possible that the recession reduced expected earnings and led to a decline in home purchases. But they conclude, "While highly skilled young workers have traditionally provided a vital influx of new, affluent consumers to US housing and auto markets, unprecedented student debt may dampen their influence in today's marketplace."

It is easy to see how this statement from Federal Reserve researchers might be taken as conclusive evidence that increases in student debt have caused young people to stop buying houses.

But a closer look at the relationship between student debt and home ownership, using data from the Federal Reserve's Survey of Consumer Finances, found that during the years before 2003, the year the Federal Reserve comparison began, people between the ages of 28 and 32 were more likely to own homes if they did not have student debt. In other words, the relatively lower home ownership rates of those who have borrowed for college are not a new phenomenon. The years between 2004 and 2011 were an exception to a long-term pattern.[17]

This analysis also raises the important question of changes in the pattern of who has student debt and who does not. If we see that people with student debt are less likely to buy houses in 2013 than they were in 2003, and we also see that average student debt balances are higher, we might conclude that it is the rise in student debt that caused the decline in home ownership. But many more people now have student debt. As detailed in Chap. 2, the characteristics of the people going to college have changed—with those changes most pronounced during the recession.

A whole segment of people who were in the non-borrower category before have shifted to the borrower category. And these are people who are not in a strong position to buy houses. It may not be that people who would have bought houses before are no longer buying them because they have debt. Rather, many people who are not likely homeowners did not go to college at all before, but because of the weak economy—and because of the increasing difficulty of getting a good job without any postsecondary education as well as the wide availability of student loans—now go to college and have student debt. They are on the other side of the line when we compare those with student debt to those without.

A recent study looked at a national sample of individual 25- and 30-year-olds. Among homeowners, 71% had some college education. Among non-homeowners, 59% had at least some college. This study does find a negative association between amounts of student debt and homeownership and mortgage sizes, but the effects—which are larger for blacks than for whites—are not large. The authors conclude, "Although we do find a very modest association between debt and home ownership, we find little evidence that student loan debt is a 'major culprit' of declining home ownership among young adults. Instead, it is likely that declining home ownership among young adults—which predates the recent rise in student loan debt—is more responsive to structural changes in the economy and changes in the transition to adulthood."[18]

Similarly, according to research from Zillow, "Yes, First-Time Buyer Demand is Weak. But Stop Blaming Student Debt,"[19] higher levels of education are associated with higher levels of home ownership. Those with no college degree of any kind are least likely to own a home, and among them, those with college debt but no degree have the lowest home ownership rates. The study found that finishing a bachelor's degree prevents borrowers from being negatively affected by student debt when it comes to buying a home. There is a marked negative relationship between amounts of student debt and home ownership for individuals with no college degree at all, a smaller relationship for those with associate degrees, and minimal relationship for those with bachelor's degrees or higher—who have significantly higher home ownership rates than individuals with lower levels of educational attainment. Graduates with advanced degrees are the most likely to own a home, even if they racked up a lot of student debt.

For households with a doctorate, master's, bachelor's, or associate degree, the proportion of buyers to renters remains relatively constant at varying levels of student debt. Unlike student debt, age, family structure, and income turn out to be very important determinants of home ownership in the Zillow study. According to the US Census, 72% of families are homeowners, compared to 50% of non-family households; 75% of households with incomes at or above the median own their homes, compared to 49% of those below the median; and 70% of households headed by 45- to 54-year-olds own homes, compared to 36% of those under the age of 35.[20]

There are occasional voices in the media arguing against the flood of weakly grounded conclusions. For example, an article in *Fortune* argued that "Rising tuition costs may be a problem, but not for the housing market." The article raised the concern discussed above about correlation and causation. The facts that the home ownership rate has fallen and that student debt has increased have led to headlines such as "Your Student Loan is Killing the Housing Market." But, the author argues, other factors could be in play. Young people are postponing many decisions about marriage, children, and settling down—whether or not they have student loans. And typical student loan debts are not really so high. The monthly payments involved surely make a difference, but they pale next to mortgage obligations—and next to the earnings premium resulting from a college education. Rising student loan debt, according to the author, may be a problem, but it is not the cause of the weak housing market.[21]

Perceptions versus Reality

A weakness of many of the studies attempting to determine the impact of student debt is that they are based on aggregate data instead of information about individuals. Student debt has gone up. New home purchases and the number of new businesses have gone down. But really understanding the relationship requires knowing about individual characteristics. Student debt affects people in different circumstances differently.

Moreover, some of the general sense of the impact of student debt on home ownership and other major life steps comes from surveys. The Gallup-Purdue poll cited above for its impact on impressions about the relationship between student debt and new business formation is one example. The same survey found that alumni who say they had supportive relationships with faculty members and mentors while they were in college are more likely than others to say college was worth the cost. They are also less likely to say that student debt has interfered with life decisions such as going to graduate school or starting a business. The report concludes from this correlation that universities—by increasing engagement among students—can influence the extent to which debt "prevents them from pursuing post-graduation goals."[22]

It is worth trying to sort through the logic here. Is it really possible that because a student feels better about her college education, her student debt will interfere less with her ability to get a mortgage or find financing for a business start-up venture? Might it be that people who strongly agree on one survey question are more likely to strongly agree on others? Might it be that people who don't think their college education was worth it have negative attitudes that color the extent to which they blame student debt for any problems they are having?

More generally, failing to differentiate between perceptions of impact and empirical evidence of impact can lead to serious misinterpretation of survey findings. People who don't succeed—for whatever reason—in accomplishing some of the things they aspire to are looking for explanations and when prompted by a survey with a plausible story may check the box without fully analyzing the actual forces affecting their outcomes.

In the specific case of student debt, surveys of borrowers in repayment in the 1990s and early 2000s documented sharp differences in the extent to which respondents reported their debt affecting home ownership, marriage, and other life choices and the actual differences in patterns among those with and without significant levels of debt. People consistently report that they believe there are larger impacts than those that emerge from actual data on outcomes.[23]

It is not easy to formulate the right question to ask about the impact of student debt—much less to find the right data and perform a reliable and convincing analysis.

It is obvious that having less money leads to lower levels of consumption, investment in housing, and saving. The question is whether the impact of student debt is different from the impact of just having less money.

Is it different to have $30,000 in student debt as opposed to $30,000 less in net worth in another form? If an experimenter gave two identical adults with the same amount of outstanding student debt a gift, with one receiving $20,000 in cash and the other receiving student loan forgiveness of $20,000, would the latter be better off? Would the absence of student debt make him or her more likely to buy a house or start a business? Or would the two individuals respond similarly to the windfall? Is it really the student debt that changes opportunities and behaviors—or is it weak financial circumstances more generally?

Student Debt and the Alternatives

Some examples of studies of causation described earlier in this chapter involve the introduction of new money. A wealthy donor or a large foundation may fund an experiment to learn more about how individuals will respond to being given additional funding. Some studies specifically focused on student debt are similar, and they do tend to find positive outcomes when students are relieved of the burden of debt. For example, Rothstein and Rouse (2011) examined the changes that occurred when a large, highly selective private university replaced loans with grants for its students. The authors found that the elimination of loans reduced the frequency with which graduates chose higher-salary jobs and increased the likelihood of entering lower-paying public service occupations.

This natural experiment provides convincing evidence of causation and of the impact of student loans on this particular population. But there is no good public policy analogy. The university used a portion of its more than ample wealth to fund this change. It is not clear what the alternative use of the funds might have been. Surely if we could give students more money without raising taxes and without giving up other valuable expenditures, they would have more options and would be better off.

No one would trade the education they got at someone else's expense for a heap of student debt. But many people who find themselves unemployable or eligible only for low-paying jobs because of a lack of education and training might willingly incur a modest amount of debt if it significantly improved their labor market opportunities.

From society's perspective, the immediate gain to students of replacing debt with public subsidies must be evaluated in the context of the transfer of resources from other social purposes and of increased tax burdens, both on former students and on individuals who have not themselves had the opportunity to obtain postsecondary education.

Too much of the critique of student debt assumes that if debt is reduced there is someone in the background ready and willing to step in and cover the costs that would otherwise be covered by that debt. That someone could be parents, if they have that kind of resources, or the government, if taxpayers are willing to foot the bill. But if there is no friendly agent waiting in the background to step in place of borrowing, then for many students the way to avoid debt will be to avoid college, and that is often a very bad choice.

Notes

1. Bureau of Labor Statistics, "Data Bases, Tables, and Calculators by Subject," accessed November 15, 2015, http://data.bls.gov/timeseries/LNS14000000.
2. Statistic Brain Research Institute, "Home Foreclosure Statistics," accessed November 2, 2015, http://www.statisticbrain.com/home-foreclosure-statistics/.
3. See, e.g. Joshua Angrist, Philip Oreopoulos, and Tyler Williams, "When Opportunity Knocks, Who Answers?" *Journal of Human Resources*, 49(3:2014): 572–610; Reshma Patel et al., "Performance-Based Scholarships: What Have We Learned?" MDRC Policy Brief, 2013; Doug Harris and Sara Goldrick-Rab, "Improving the Productivity of Education Experiments: Lessons from a Randomized Study of Need-Based Financial Aid." *Educational Finance and Policy*, 7(2:2012); 143–169.
4. Timothy Bartik, Brad Hershbein, and Marta Lachowska, "The Effects of the Kalamazoo Promise Scholarship on College Enrollment, Persistence, and Completion," W.E. Upjohn Institute for Employment, Research Working Paper 15–229, 2015; Susan Dynarski, "Does Aid Matter? Measuring The Effect Of Student Aid On College Attendance And Completion," *American Economic Review*, 93 (1:2003): 279–288; Susan Dynarski, "Hope for Whom? Financial Aid for the Middle Class and Its Impact on College Attendance," *National Tax Journal*, 53(3:2000): 629–661; Thomas Kane, "Evaluating the Impact of the D.C. Tuition Assistance Grant Program." *Journal of Human Resources*, 42(3:2007).
5. Sandy Baum, Diane Elliott, and Jennifer Ma, *Trends in Student Aid 2014* (New York: The College Board, 2014), Figure 14B.
6. Richard Fry, "Young Adults, Student Debt, and Economic Well-Being," Pew Research Center, 2014, http://www.pewsocialtrends.org/2014/05/14/young-adults-student-debt-and-economic-well-being/.
7. Chana Shoenberger, "Want to be an entrepreneur? Beware of student debt," *Wall Street Journal*, May 26, 2015, http://www.wsj.com/articles/want-to-be-an-entrepreneur-beware-of-student-debt-1432318500.
8. Brent Ambrose, Larry Cordell, and Shuwei Ma, "The Impact of Student Loan Debt on Small Business Formation," *Social Science Research Network*, July 15, 2015, http://ssrn.com/abstract=2417676.

9. Gallup and Purdue University, *Great Jobs, Great Lives: The Relationship Between Student Debt, Experiences, and Perceptions of College Worth.* Gallup Purdue Index 2015 Report (Washington, DC: Gallup, 2015), http://www.gallup.com/services/185888/gallup-purdue-index-report-2015.aspx.
10. Brandon Busteed, "Student Loan Debt: Major Barrier to Entrepreneurship," *Business Journal,* October 14, 2015, http://www.gallup.com/businessjournal/186179/student-loan-debt-major-barrier-entrepreneurship.aspx.
11. Chana Shoenberger, "Want to be an Entrepreneur? Beware of Student Debt."
12. Scott Shane, "Is Student Debt the Reason Millennials Aren't Starting Companies?" *Entrepreneur*, August 3, 2015, http://www.entrepreneur.com/article/249036.
13. Sandy Baum, "Does Increasing Reliance on Student Debt Explain Declines in Entrepreneurial Activity?" The Urban Institute, 2015, http://www.urban.org/research/publication/does-increasing-reliance-student-debt-explain-declines-entrepreneurial-activity.
14. Federal Reserve Bank of New York, *Quarterly Report on Household Debt and Credit*, November 2015, https://www.newyorkfed.org/medialibrary/interactives/householdcredit/data/pdf/HHDC_2015Q3.pdf.
15. Federal Reserve Bank of New York, "Household Credit," accessed November 25, 2015, http://www.newyorkfed.org/regional/householdcredit.html.
16. Meta Brown and Sydnee Caldwell, "Young Adult Student Loan Borrowers Retreat from Housing and Auto Markets," (New York: Federal Reserve Bank of New York, 2013), http://libertystreeteconomics.newyorkfed.org/2013/04/young-student-loan-borrowers-retreat-from-housing-and-auto-markets.html#.VbpQIipViko.
17. Beth Akers, "Reconsidering the Conventional Wisdom on Student Debt and Home Ownership," Brookings Institution, Brown Center Chalkboard, May 8, 2014, http://www.brookings.edu/research/papers/2014/05/08-student-loan-debt-and-home-ownership-akers.
18. Jason Houle and Lawrence Berger, *The End of the American Dream? Student Loan Debt and Home Ownership Among Young Adults* (Washington, DC: Third Way, 2015), http://www.thirdway.org/report/the-end-of-the-american-dream-student-loan-debt-and-homeownership-among-young-adults.
19. Jamie Anderson, "Yes, First-Time Buyer Demand is Weak. But Stop Blaming Student Debt." *Zillow Real Estate Resear*ch, September 16, 2015,http://www.zillow.com/research/student-debt-homeownership-10563/; Melissa Allison, "Student Debt has Minor Effect on Homeownership—As Long As You Get a Four-Year Degree," September 16, 2015, http://www.zillow.com/blog/student-debt-effect-homeownership-182547/.

20. Jonathan Vespa, Jamie Lewis and Rose Kreider, *America's Families and Living Arrangements, 2012*, (Washington, DC: U.S. Census Bureau, 2013), P20-570; Robert Callis and Melssa Kresin, *Residential Vacancies and Homeownership in the Third Quarter 2015*, U.S. Census Bureau News, October 27, 2015.
21. Chris Matthews, "Student loan debt is not hurting America's housing market," *Fortune,* July 27, 2015, http://fortune.com/2015/07/27/student-loan-debt-housing/.
22. Gallup and Purdue University, *Great Jobs, Great Lives.*
23. Sandy Baum and Saul Schwartz, *The Impact of Student Loans on Borrowers: Consumption Patterns and Attitudes Towards Repayment*, (Boston: Massachusetts Higher Education Assistance Corporation, 1988); Sandy Baum and Diane Saunders, "Life After Debt: Results of the National Student Loan Survey," (Boston: Nellie Mae, 1998); Sandy Baum, *College on Credit: How Borrowers Perceive their Education Debt*, (Boston: Nellie Mae, 2003).

CHAPTER 5

How Can Public Policy Help?

Abstract The most important strategy for ameliorating student debt problems is preventing people from borrowing for programs they are unlikely to complete and institutions that won't serve them well. There should also be stricter limits on borrowing for graduate students, parents, and some undergraduates. Major steps for dealing with existing debt include an improved income-driven payment system that appropriately supports borrowers while expecting most to repay their debts in full and improving the structures surrounding the repayment and collection processes—but not forgiving all or most debt. Other promising policy changes include easing the restrictions on discharging student debt in bankruptcy, eliminating the privileged category of private student loans, and making it easier for students to borrow less than the maximum allowed.

Keywords Student debt • College financing • Income-driven repayment • Debt forgiveness

The generic discussion of a student loan "crisis"—considering all borrowing for college an unmitigated evil and viewing those obliged to repay student debt as victims of an oppressive system—has the potential to discourage people from going to college even if it would significantly improve their lives. The alarmist narrative also distracts from the serious problems with student debt

S. Baum, *Student Debt*, DOI 10.1057/978-1-137-52738-7_5

that could be addressed without totally transforming the system of higher education finance or arbitrarily and disproportionately shifting burdens from the people who benefit most from higher education to taxpayers in general.

There are problems, but they are different from the problems that many policy proposals are designed to address.

It is a problem that students are borrowing to enroll in colleges and programs from which they are unlikely to graduate and/or which, even if they do graduate, are not likely to lead to positive labor market outcomes.

It is a problem that many recent college graduates (and non-graduates) have entered the labor force while the economy is weak, unemployment is high, and opportunities are scarce.

It is a problem that state disinvestment in higher education has led to rapidly rising tuition levels in public colleges at a time when families are struggling to make ends meet and are not in a good position to pay for their children's education. The combination of higher tuition and diminished family support has contributed to rapid increases in borrowing.

It is a problem that the USA has not created or funded a strong workforce development system. Too many adults find that their only hope for finding a good job is to go back to school. These adult students borrow large amounts, partly because they enroll disproportionately in expensive for-profit colleges and partly because they are borrowing to support themselves and their families while they are in school. In the absence of strong apprenticeship or workplace-based training programs, reasonable support for job training that does not involve borrowing, and a strong safety net for individuals and families with inadequate labor market earnings, too many people are making questionable decisions about borrowing money to go back to school.

It is also a problem that the federal student loan system does not place reasonable limits on the amount graduate students and parents of dependent students can borrow.

These problems involve student debt. But they do not imply that the majority of people who have gone to college are suffering "crushing" student debt. They do not imply that individuals with student debt are, overall, among the most financially strained groups in the nation. They do not imply that borrowing to finance an investment in higher education is a self-destructive decision. And they do not imply that public policy should be focused either on forgiving the debt of most of those who have borrowed for education or on preventing students from having to borrow in the future.

Addressing the real problems in student debt requires a dispassionate assessment of policies that have already been implemented, of policies that are currently under discussion, and of other potential approaches. The goals include alleviating the burden of borrowers who are in untenable situations and, of particular importance, reducing the number of students who, in the future, take loans they are unlikely to be able to repay with reasonable effort.

But the goals should also include ensuring that future students are comfortable borrowing reasonable amounts of money to invest in their futures and taking responsibility for repaying those loans; that taxpayers provide ample and well-targeted subsidies designed to increase educational opportunities; and that students and families—as well as postsecondary institutions and society at large—take responsibility both for financing higher education and for strengthening its quality and the proportion of students who succeed in improving their lives through education.

Should Subsidizing Student Borrowers Be at the Top of the Social Agenda?

As discussed in Chap. 1, people owing education debt are not the worst off members of our society Many people, particularly those with lower levels of educational attainment, face bigger challenges. And as noted in Chap. 3, our nation faces many challenges that beg for more public funding. These are not arguments against support for colleges and universities and their students or excuses for failing to adequately protect students for whom postsecondary education does not pay off as well as they could reasonably have expected. Rather, they are arguments for viewing problems with student debt as specific rather than general. Solutions should be targeted to address the very real problems some students face as a result of the high price of college and limited economic opportunities and support systems.

The starting point for developing the best possible student loan policies is an understanding of their purpose. As discussed earlier, loans provide liquidity to people who don't have the cash up front, but can expect lifetime earnings that will be more than adequate to pay for postsecondary education. The government is involved primarily because the absence of credit histories and collateral means that the private market would either deny credit to or demand unsatisfactory terms of the borrowers struggling most to pay for their education. The discussion below focuses first on preventing unproductive borrowing—probably the most important step for the long run. It then moves to management of existing student loan borrowers, dividing the policy options into those that would be major structural changes and those that are targeted changes that could be made more easily but still have the potential to ease the problems facing many borrowers, while preserving the integrity of the taxpayer-funded system.

The student loan issue is not monolithic. Graduate students face issues that are quite different from those faced by typical undergraduates. The circumstances of most older students, enrolling in college after having been in the labor force for a number of years and frequently having dependents of their own, are quite different from those of recent high school graduates. Students borrowing to attend for-profit institutions are particularly vulnerable. And perhaps most important, too many students borrow for college when they have little chance of completing their programs. As discussed earlier, default rates among non-completers are much higher than those for graduates and many borrowers struggle even with relatively small balances.

The prevalence of non-completion would be a serious problem even absent student loans. It is too often a sign of wasted time, effort, and money, in addition to shattered dreams. But arguing that debt finance is inappropriate because some people do not complete credentials is not logical. We urgently need stronger pre-college academic preparation, better guidance about choosing schools and programs, better policing of postsecondary quality, and better student support systems. We should minimize the number of students who enroll in programs they are not likely to complete, not just ensure that they don't borrow excessively to fund these dead-end paths. We are much more likely to be able to fund these efforts amply if we carefully target public subsidies to those who need them. Because most students experience significant financial benefits from their college education, most of them can repay loans. We should not direct our limited dollars away from the more urgent needs to repaying loans for people with high levels of education and high earnings potential.

Preventing Problems

The New York Times ran an article in *The Upshot* that featured a high school teacher who owes the government $410,000 in education debt. This extraordinary circumstance arose from the combination of a series of very bad decisions and some very bad luck. After 25 years of borrowing, this 48-year-old woman has apparently not made any payments on any of her federal loans. Much of the amount she now owes represents unpaid interest, but she did receive something over $200,000 to help her pay her bills.[1] It is impossible to argue that this atypical situation is an unavoidable one that just requires policies for more easily writing off debt. It should be impossible for people to get into this situation—or at least the federal government should never facilitate this outcome. The federal government is partly responsible, but surely the borrower also bears some responsibility.

Before delving more into the details of policies relating to the management of debt, we should address the question of how we can limit problematic borrowing. Isolating the types of education borrowing that are most likely to lead to difficulties and stopping these mistakes before they happen while still encouraging people to invest in themselves and their futures, even if that means incurring debt, is a better solution than arguing that education debt is always "good" debt—or trying to eliminate student debt.

Excluding Institutions That Don't Serve Students Well

As a society, we should be able to provide the funding required to prevent young people from low-income backgrounds from borrowing significant sums of money to prepare for occupations unlikely to lead to careers that can reasonably support debt payments. For example, many students borrow to study cosmetology, a career with a median wage of about $23,000 a year.[2] Not surprisingly, four of the eight schools on the list of institutions subject to loss of Direct Loan Program and/or Federal Pell Grant Program eligibility due to fiscal year 2010, 2011, and 2012 official three-year default rates of 30% or higher are cosmetology schools.[3] Clearly, we need people trained to perform these services, but the current training structure is not viable.

More generally, continuing to award federal student aid for institutions that serve very few of their students well is irresponsible. The rules for losing eligibility for federal student aid are so loose that schools are rarely disqualified. As the *New York Times* pointed out, "For-Profit Colleges Accused of Fraud Still Receive US Funds."[4] Many students' lives are being severely damaged because they enroll in schools with very low graduation rates, high student loan default rates, and little promise of success.

The federal government hands students grants and loans and allows them to attend these institutions—where they borrow and later predictably default. Whether they are for-profit institutions, community colleges, or other public or private nonprofit colleges and universities, these institutions must be more firmly regulated. Prohibiting them from operating may be questionable, but funding them through student aid dollars is bad for the taxpayers and bad for the students who receive the aid.

The federal government is attempting to address this issue through the implementation of "Gainful Employment" regulations. These regulations apply to almost all programs at for-profit institutions and to all non-degree programs, including certificate programs, offered by public and private nonprofit institutions. After years of legal challenges by the for-profit industry and an adverse court ruling, the Department of Education implemented rules in July 2015 that will disqualify from the federal student aid system programs whose graduates have average debt payments exceeding specified percentages of their incomes. This approach is an important step, but it is not strong enough to solve the problem. One obvious shortcoming is that the criteria focus only on graduates, not the many students who enroll in these programs but never complete credentials.

Helping Students Make Better Choices

With or without stricter regulation, students need better guidance and more restrictions on their borrowing. We should effectively advise a student who is seeking a master's degree in history at a non-elite institution to borrow less than the amount that would be manageable for a student who has been accepted to a top law school. With current technology and with a small fraction of the resources the federal government devotes to postsecondary students, we could provide strong and personalized advice. It is not enough to expect colleges and universities to provide this advice to their students.

Moreover, the way options are presented can have a significant impact on the choices people make. We know, for example, that in many situations people take the path of least resistance, accepting whatever path requires least action.[5] Making it easier for students to opt for smaller loans and requiring more active steps to borrow the maximum allowed could make a real difference.

A Comprehensive Strategy for Limiting Overborrowing

A constructive approach must include several elements:

1. Stricter rules for institutional eligibility for federal student aid programs.
2. Stronger incentives for institutions to improve their performance and reduce the debt levels of their students, possibly through a system that

forces institutions to bear part of the financial risk when their students do not repay their loans.[6]

3. Better guidance for students making decisions about what, where, when, and with what intensity to pursue postsecondary studies, with systems tailored for the differing needs of recent high school graduates and older adults returning to school.
4. More nuanced loan limits that permit part-time students to borrow less than full-time students and allow institutions to provide federal loans without offering all students loans up to the legal maximum regardless of their circumstances.
5. Strict limits on the Grad PLUS and Parent PLUS programs, ending the practice of allowing graduate students and parents of undergraduates to borrow up to the full cost of attendance (including tuition, fees, room, board, and other expenses) less grant aid—no matter how high those costs.
6. Better tracking of student success across institutions so they do not borrow for an unsuccessful course of study at one school and then move on to a different school and accumulate more debt without showing any progress toward a credential.

All of these constructive approaches specific to student loans will be of limited value if we don't solve the more fundamental problems. Students who are academically prepared for college are more likely to succeed, to earn credentials, and to be able to repay their loans. Strengthening the education system from early childhood through high school is a key part of improving college outcomes—including those pertaining to student debt.

No matter how strong their credentials, students graduating into a weak economy are likely to face hurdles on the path to well-paying careers. The coincidence of the Great Recession and the prominence of student debt as a concern is not an accident. A stronger economy, higher wages, and less income inequality—with less purchasing power at the top and more in the middle and lower ranges of the income distribution—would reduce the number of former students struggling to pay off their education debt.

If tuition were lower, because of some combination of lower costs of operation and stronger public funding for higher education institutions, and need-based grant aid that does not have to be repaid were more available, students would face smaller gaps between their expenses and their ability to pay. And if the federal government put stricter limits on the amounts older undergraduates and particularly graduate student are allowed to borrow, students would accumulate less education debt and repayment would be less of a problem.

Is Information Enough?

Some proposals for improving student outcomes and mitigating problems with student debt rely on the idea that with enough information, students will make better choices. The basic idea is that we don't need a lot of regulation of institutions or limits on borrowing. Market forces will lead to optimal outcomes as people make the choices that maximize their long-run well-being.

But in reality, good information about postsecondary options is necessary but not sufficient to minimize the mismatch between students and programs that leads to a significant portion of the problems borrowers experience with education debt.

There is no doubt that better information and more personalized counseling could help students to make better borrowing decisions. In 2007, when private student loans were more prevalent than they are now, Barnard College implemented a policy of having a conversation with each family before certifying their daughters' enrollment to give them access to private student loans. The College did not refuse to certify students. It just provided information about the differences between private and federal student loans and some of the risks involved in the former. More than half of the families decided against taking these loans after they learned more about them.[7]

But expecting borrowers to respond to market signals is likely to be less effective. In an effort to encourage students to make better decisions about enrollment in and financing of postsecondary education, some proposals focus on "risk-rating" of student loans. Crawford and Sheets (2013), for example, argue that interest rates (as well as loan limits) should be pegged to the expected earnings of students. Risk assessment would be based on the institution and the particular program, in addition to the student's characteristics. They argue that this approach would reward students for working hard to become college-ready and nudge them to choose more promising programs where they would be able to borrow at lower interest rates.[8]

But many students have no idea what the interest rates on their loans are. They frequently don't know whether they have federal loans or private loans, and if they have federal loans, whether they are subsidized, with the government paying the interest while they are in school, or unsubsidized with interest accruing. In fact, a startling number of student borrowers do not even know that they have borrowed funds they will have to repay.[9]

Preventing students from accumulating large amount of debt they are unlikely to be able to repay will take more than information about institutions and their outcomes and market signals from the terms on student loans.

Managing Existing Debt: Big Ideas

Over the long term, policy changes that will prevent unmanageable debt are better solutions than those that just relieve the problems after they materialize. Once a student borrows for an unproductive path or incurs disproportionate debt for a successful course of study, letting the borrower off the hook inevitably passes the burden on to taxpayers. But we also have to address the challenges facing borrowers who are already in untenable situations and those who will slip through the cracks and get into these situations in the future. Moreover, the variation in outcomes among individuals with similar characteristics enrolling in similar programs requires well-designed policies providing insurance against unanticipated unfavorable outcomes.

Some of the policy ideas below are big ideas. Those ideas will be difficult to implement but deserve long-term attention. Other ideas are more focused and should be feasible without major overhaul of the college financing system.

Improve Income-Driven Repayment

It is discouraging, to say the least, to hear presidential candidates trying to get attention for their proposals to solve the student debt problem by letting students repay in accord with their incomes. The problem is not that this is a bad idea. The problem is that we have such a system in place. Either the candidates are unaware of it or they are just counting on the electorate to be unaware. The system could be strengthened. The premise is a good one. But the system as implemented in the USA to date has not solved the prevailing problems. We should be asking why not, rather than pretending the concept has not already been put into practice.

Better information about and easier access to income-driven repayment plans are important steps. Currently, many borrowers who could benefit are unaware of the option and others complain that their loan servicers do not facilitate the process or they encounter other bureaucratic problems.[10]

But careful structuring of income-driven repayment is also important. The Obama administration has taken a number of steps to increase the generosity of the program for borrowers. Instead of expecting borrowers to make payments equal to 15% of the part of the their incomes that exceeds 150% of the poverty line for their family size, new provisions lower that rate to 10%. Instead of forgiving unpaid balances after 25 years, new provisions lower that time period to 20 years.[11]

The goal of income-driven repayment is to ensure that borrowers who experience fluctuations in their incomes, whose education does not pay off as well as anticipated, or who experience other unforeseen adversity are not overwhelmed by their obligations. But that is different from making payment obligations as low as possible.

There are too many details involved in designing an income-driven repayment system to go into all of them here. But a couple of simple examples will clarify the problem. In 2015, the poverty level for a single individual was $11,770. So a single borrower participating in income-driven repayment would not be required to make monthly payments until his or her income exceeded $17,655—150% of the poverty level. For a borrower earning $25,000 a year, the change from 15% to 10% would lower monthly payments from $92 to $61. For a borrower earning $50,000 a year, payments would fall from $404 per month to $270. In other words, the larger benefits go to the higher earners.

Lowering both the repayment rate and the time until the debt is forgiven means more borrowers will end up not paying off their entire debts. Designing a strong system requires careful thinking about under what circumstances it is appropriate for debt to be forgiven.[12] It also requires avoiding a situation where institutions can charge unlimited prices and students can borrow unlimited amounts knowing that high debt levels will not increase the total payments they make.

Make Repayment Easier

The process of repaying is too frequently burdensome regardless of the size of the required payments. It is not always easy for loan servicers to keep track of borrowers, who tend to move frequently in the years following college. There are frequent complaints about whether payments are credited in a timely manner and how they are allocated when a borrower has multiple loans. The repayment system would be much simpler for borrowers if it operated through income tax withholding, as it does in some other countries. This change is an integral part of many proposals for making income-driven repayment the standard for all borrowers.

In addition to making the process easier for borrowers, using withholding to collect student loan payments would put student loan payments at the top of the priority list for expenditures. It is quite reasonable that borrowers choosing between making their student loan payments and their car payments choose the latter—they stand to lose their cars for missed payments, but the consequences of missing student loan payments are both less concrete and more remote. It would not be surprising if many other expenditures—some of which could surely be described as discretionary—also move ahead of student loans in many borrowers' budgets. Under a withholding system, while payment would always be in line with incomes, borrowers would have limited options for making those payments a low priority.

Don't Forgive All Student Debt!

The idea of forgiving all outstanding student debt is not likely to gain widespread support anytime soon, but it has gotten enough attention to make it worth addressing. The concept that student debt is an unmitigated evil, that no one should be expected to borrow to finance their education, leads some observers to conclude that the best solution would be to forgive all outstanding student debt. In order to be in any way equitable, or to be a long-term solution, this debt forgiveness would have to be accompanied by policies that would ensure that no students ever borrow again.

A typical argument is that "it is time to break the chains that student loan debt has placed on a generation of young people… [We] have created a 'lost generation' of debt-saddled, young people lost not only to themselves but unable to help build a more vibrant country." The solution is a Jubilee of Debt Forgiveness that "would trigger an American Renaissance of young people free to be creative, take risks, explore ideas and lives without owing a pound of flesh to the banks."[13]

Forgiving all student is such a misguided idea that it is hard to know where to begin. If the federal government were to announce tomorrow that all outstanding student loan balances have been reduced to zero, how would those who have just finished repaying their debts feel? Could a policy that would neglect those who have met their obligations but provide a handout to those who have not possibly be either equitable or efficient?

Because, as noted in Chap. 1, households in the top quartile of the income distribution owe a disproportionate amount of student debt, they would reap a disproportionate amount of the benefits if all education debt were forgiven. If this seems counterintuitive, just think about the incomes of people who went to college and stayed in college long enough to borrow a lot of money—compared to the incomes of those who never went to college and thus have no education debt. Higher levels of debt are associated with more years in school and more advanced degrees. More education is associated with higher earnings. So borrowers with large debts include many doctors, lawyers, and business executives. It's hard to see how forgiving their debt would make the world a fairer place.

Surely there are borrowers whose outstanding debt *should* be forgiven. As discussed below, trying to collect from people who are permanently disabled, retired and living on Social Security, or have declared bankruptcy is ethically questionable in addition to being inefficient. But as with most of the discussion of student debt, it is important not to paint with a broad brush. Most borrowers can and should repay their debts.

Managing Existing Debt: Easier Fixes

While big ideas are probably needed to ensure a stable higher education funding system for the future, some small fixes could make a real difference. Most of the visible horror stories of student debt are examples of specific problems affecting a relatively small number of borrowers—problems that might be eliminated without overhauling the entire system.

Is Lowering All Interest Rates Really a Good Idea?

Probably the most common suggestion for easing the burden on borrowers is to lower the interest rates they are charged. Sen. Elizabeth Warren (D-MA) made this issue a high priority, arguing that the federal government is making money off of students by charging interest rates higher than the rate at which the government itself borrows. Despite controversy over the most appropriate way to measure the cost of loans to the government,[14] a number of members of Congress as well as presidential candidates from both parties have picked up on the idea as a viable solution to easing the problems of student debt borrowers.

But as the information cited above about higher-income households owing more in student debt than lower-income households makes clear, the benefits of this policy are likely to be poorly targeted. Moreover, the monthly payments of borrowers participating in income-driven repayment plans are not affected by the interest rates on their loans. Only the time to full repayment and the amount eventually forgiven for those who never completely repay would be affected by having their loans refinanced at lower interest rates.

However, under the current system, borrowers who happened to take out loans in years when the interest rates on student loans were high owe more than similar borrowers who happened to borrow in a lower-interest rate environment. Many individual borrowers have loans at a variety of different interest rates. A solution to this problem would be to issue variable rate loans. When interest rates are low, all borrowers would pay low interest rates—or accrue interest at a low rate; when market rates are high, student loan borrowers, like others, would pay higher rates.

It is important to note that despite the impression given by much of the discussion of student loan refinancing, borrowers are not in any way blocked from or penalized for refinancing their loans. A number of private companies are in the business of refinancing student loans. Any borrower is free to look for a lower interest rate than that charged by the government. But not surprisingly, it is borrowers who are not struggling who are most able to take advantage of this opportunity. Creditors are interested in lending to borrowers with strong credit ratings, valuable credentials, and good prospects for remunerative careers. The market will not address the needs of borrowers most at risk of not being able to repay their debts.

Don't Let So Much Unpaid Interest Accumulate

Some of the more heartbreaking stories about student debt involve people who borrowed relatively small amounts of money but have seen their debts balloon as a result of unpaid interest accruing and fees or penalties being applied. *The New York Times* reported the story of Rosemary Anderson, a 57-year-old woman, with a home mortgage that is under water, as well as health and other problems, and $64,000 in unpaid student loans. She borrowed more than 20 years ago to fund her bachelor's and master's degrees, but fell behind on the payments. As a result of compound interest, her debt has risen to $126,000. She estimates that she will be 81 by the time the debt is retired, and will have paid $87,487 more than she originally borrowed.[15]

We don't know why Rosemary fell behind on her loan payments to start with, but we do know that accruing unpaid interest can lead to snowballing problems. If you borrow $10,000 at an interest rate of 4%

and are scheduled to pay it back with fixed payments over ten years, you will owe $101 each month. In the first month, $33 will cover interest and the rest will reduce the principal. If you made your payments steadily for two years, you would find yourself with a debt of $8306 and the interest in the first month of your third year of payments would have fallen to $28. But if you don't make any payments, and the unpaid interest is added to your debt each month, you will owe $10,795 at the beginning of the third year, and your next month's interest charge will be $36.[16] A higher debt or a higher interest rate would exacerbate your problem.

It is not unreasonable that interest accrues on unpaid debts. It works that way with most debts. But if we are looking for ways to diminish the burden on people whose educations did not pay off as expected, this is not a bad place to start. If Rosemary can't manage to pay her original debt, it's hard to imagine that she is going to end up paying off all of this accrued interest. Under current law, she is unlikely to be able to discharge the debt in bankruptcy proceedings. If she enrolls in an income-driven repayment plan, she is likely to have her remaining balances forgiven after 20 or 25 years. She will have had the extra debt hanging over her head for all that time, but she won't pay it either way.

Limiting the amount of unpaid interest that is added to debt balances—while ensuring that borrowers in this situation do not keep borrowing additional funds they will never repay—may, therefore, be a relatively low-cost way to limit the number of people facing impossible student debt burdens.

Don't Garnish Social Security Payments

There are also distressing stories about senior citizens living on Social Security and seeing their payments garnished for long-unpaid student debts. This is not a problem that affects many people. In 2010, 3% of households (706,000) headed by individuals ages 65 and older reported having student debt. Households in this age range were much more likely to have credit card debt and home mortgages. But the education debt in this age group is growing and in 2013, the federal government withheld Social Security benefits from 155,000 recipients, including 36,000 over the age of 65—and many younger people who lost some of their benefit payments.[17]

We don't know why these older people never repaid their debts. Almost 20% of the education debt among older adults is from the Parent PLUS program. Some of these loans were taken out not so long ago to pay for children's education. The borrowers knew they were close to retirement.

Some borrowers may have failed to repay despite having the resources to do so because they believed they shouldn't have to pay for college, because they felt their education wasn't worth it, or simply because they had other priorities. But it seems likely that most of these borrowers didn't pay because of financial struggles. And they are unlikely to be in a position to pay after they retire.

Current policy allows for the federal student loans of people with documented total and permanent disability to be forgiven.[18] It appears, however, that differences in definitions or other bureaucratic issues lead to the garnishing of some Social Security disability payments. It should not be difficult to solve this problem.

Older individuals are a little more complicated, but with restrictions that would prevent people close to retirement age from borrowing and having the debt quickly forgiven because of their age, ending this practice would be another relatively low-cost way of diminishing the number of painful stories of the impact of student debt. Garnishing tax refunds or a percentage of wages is one thing. Further diminishing the living standards of senior citizens and disabled people with no potential for labor market earnings who are struggling to make ends meet on their Social Security payments is quite another thing.

Private Loans Should Not Be Called "Student Loans"

In 2014–15, undergraduate and graduate students borrowed about $10 billion from banks, Sallie Mae, and other non-federal sources.[19] Because these loans are called "student loans," many borrowers do not understand that they do not carry the same protections that come with federal student loans. The interest rates are not limited by legislation and income-driven repayment plans and other provisions for financial hardship are generally unavailable. Moreover, in many cases borrowers are forced to repay the entire debt or be declared in default if their co-signer files for bankruptcy or dies. Some of the contracts for private student loans have provisions that can create serious problems for unwitting borrowers and the Consumer Financial Protection Bureau (CFPB) has documented many other questionable practices.[20]

Why do we have such a category of loans? Students are of course free to borrow from anyone who will lend to them, to accumulate balances on their credit cards, or to use other non-optimal strategies for financing education. But there is no reason for the government to sanction these unsecured loans as student loans or to grant them any special provisions, particularly, as discussed below, protection from bankruptcy proceedings.

Treat Student Debt Like Other Debt in Bankruptcy

There are differences of opinion about how onerous the current provisions for discharging student loans in bankruptcy proceedings are. The standards are significantly higher than for other forms of consumer debt, requiring that debt can only be discharged if it imposes "undue hardship" on the borrower. Some borrowers who pursue this path do succeed in getting their loans discharged, but very few try. Part of the problem is the actual difficulty of succeeding, but part of it is surely the widespread impression that discharge is virtually impossible so it is not worth trying.[21] Clarifying the standards so more borrowers could take advantage of their rights would be a positive step.

There may be an argument for income-driven repayment plans replacing the need for bankruptcy relief in the federal student loan program. If a borrower's income is low, he or she won't be required to make payments. As long as loan forgiveness is part of the program, the debt will eventually be erased. Nonetheless, it is hard to find justification for requiring individuals with little hope of ever repaying their debts to live for years with the burden hanging over them, rather than allowing them to discharge their student loans through bankruptcy proceedings.

Until and unless we stop distinguishing between private student loans and other types of unsecured consumer debt, we can at least remove the distinction in the bankruptcy code. Why should a destitute person be able to discharge credit card debt but not debt incurred to pay for college? It is difficult to find a good argument—other than the idea that lenders might be less eager to lend to students with poor repayment prospects—which would actually be a positive outcome. Moreover, lenders would have greater incentive to be flexible about negotiating repayment terms with borrowers facing financial difficulties if they knew there was a possibility the whole debt might be wiped out.

The simplest solution is simply to eliminate the difference between student loans and other forms of credit in the bankruptcy law. Of course these provisions should be carefully designed and courts should not indiscriminately wipe out debts, but treating education debt more harshly than other forms of consumer debt is hard to justify.

Provide Lines of Credit Instead of Preset Loan Amounts

Under the current system, students sign up at the beginning of the term for a specified loan amount. The check goes to the institution and if there is anything left over after tuition and other charges are subtracted, the student gets a refund check. While these refunds can be disbursed at intervals over the term, it is common for them to be lump sum up front payments. Some experimentation is ongoing to examine the impact of spreading out the payments, treating them more like a paycheck.[22] The primary goal is to improve student success through a combination of budgeting discipline and incentives for staying in school. But there could also be an impact on borrowing levels.

Another approach might be to set up a system more analogous to a line of credit. The idea is similar to the distinction between a home equity loan for a fixed amount and a home equity line of credit. Students would not have to commit to borrowing the full amount, but could draw on their accounts as needed over the term. Experiments with this approach would determine whether it has the potential to diminish borrowing for students whose loans are covering living expenses.

Put Reasonable Limits on the Amounts Students and Parents Can Borrow

A reported case of a 65-year-old borrower seeking bankruptcy relief for federal loans he took out to finance his children's education raises more questions about loan limits than about the standards for discharging education debt. The first year he took a Parent PLUS loan the father had a $165,000 a year job. Although he lost that job a year later and had not found another one for 12 or 13 years, he continued borrowing for another 5 years.[23]

As the court debates whether the borrower is obviously incapable of paying and facing "undue hardship," or whether he is a freeloader who irresponsibly borrowed large amounts of money when he was unemployed and nearing retirement age, the fundamental question is why the federal government made these loans in the first place.

Overly stringent credit requirements on loans to parents would limit options for many middle-income families. But unlike students, parents do not expect their own incomes to rise as a result of the education they are financing. Allowing them to borrow unlimited amount of money (up to enough to cover all tuition, fees, room, board, and other living expenses not covered by grant aid) with no feasible means of repayment is not the solution. Perhaps the government should have provided more generous assistance to this family in the first place because of their precarious financial circumstances. But issuing loans knowing there is little chance they will be repaid and forgiving them for those who complain loudly enough cannot be the best solution.

Another question about loan limits relates to the difference between the amounts of federal student loans currently available to dependent students, whose parents are in the picture, and independent students, who are either age 24 or older, married, with dependents, or in other circumstances that take their parents' finances off the table. Currently, dependent students can borrow up to $31,000 in federal Stafford Subsidized and Unsubsidized loans combined over the course of their undergraduate careers. Independent students can borrow up to $57,500. The idea behind this difference is that dependent students can rely on their parents for some help. If their parents are unable to qualify for federal parent loans, they can take advantage of the higher loan limit available to independent students.

As Table 5.1 indicates, independent students are more likely than dependent students to be enrolled in low-price community colleges, but they are also more than three times as likely to attend for-profit institutions, which have significantly higher price tags than either public four-year or public two-year institutions. While private nonprofit colleges and universities have higher published tuition prices than for-profit institutions, net prices for low-income students are actually lower at private nonprofit institutions, which award significant institutional grant aid to help students pay.[24]

Perhaps loan limits should be the same, or at least more similar, for the two categories of students. Allowing independent students to borrow so much facilitates their enrollment in the for-profit sector. More of them might be induced to switch to community colleges if they could not borrow

Table 5.1 Enrollment of first-year undergraduate students by sector, 2011–12

	Public four-year	Private nonprofit four-year	Public two-year	Private for-profit	Others or attended more than one school
Dependent students	26%	12%	47%	7%	8%
Independent students	9%	3%	56%	25%	7%

Source: NCES, National Postsecondary Student Aid Study 2012

so much from the federal government. It is also likely that for-profit institutions would lower their prices if students could not borrow so much.[25] Given the lower completion rates of independent students—and the reality that when they do complete they tend to earn associate degrees and certificates that lead to lower earnings than bachelor's degrees—the generous federal loan limits surely contribute to overborrowing among this group of students.

And as mentioned above, among the most obvious targets for reform is the need for limits on the amounts that graduate students and parents of dependent students can borrow through the PLUS programs. Unlimited borrowing is a bad strategy for both taxpayers and borrowers.

Don't Tax Forgiven Loan Balances

Under current law unpaid loan balances that are forgiven through income-driven repayment programs are taxable. Borrowers whose incomes have not, over the long run, supported adequate repayment suddenly face significant income tax bills.[26] Financial advisor Suze Orman warns borrowers against income-driven repayment plans, partly because their extended time period increases total interest payments, but also because of the tax bill that is generated by any forgiven outstanding balances.[27]

Altering this policy would not make life easier for people who are in the repayment stage. But it would rationalize the system and make it more likely that borrowers' troubles end when their loan balances go to zero. It seems obvious that people who have been unable to make their loan payments are not going to be able to pay the tax bill when the debt is removed. The forgiveness doesn't put any extra money into their pockets.

The Mortgage Debt Relief Act of 2007 addressed this issue for forgiven housing debt, allowing taxpayers to exclude income from the discharge of debt on their principle residence.[28] Several bills in Congress and President Obama's 2015 budget proposal have supported eliminating the income tax on forgiven student loan balances, but this seemingly uncontroversial fix has not, to date, been implemented.[29]

Improve Loan Servicing

It would be best if we prevented people from taking out loans they are unlikely to be able to repay. Second best would be supporting borrowers with easy to navigate insurance strategies that prevent them from becoming entangled in a complex and hostile system of loan servicing for borrowers who have not made the required payments. But as long as there are struggling borrowers depending on the loan servicing system, it should not be so difficult to make that system more flexible and supportive.

Loan servicers manage borrowers' accounts, process monthly payments, manage enrollment in alternative repayment plans, and communicate directly with borrowers, including borrowers in distress. Unfortunately, in the absence of consistent federal standards, servicers have quite a bit of discretion about their practices. The CFPB collects comments from borrowers on their experiences. These are not random borrowers, but those who feel strongly enough to register their complaints, so it is hard to know how prevalent the difficulties are. But there are many complaints.

Among other things, borrowers report that servicers impose inappropriate charges, do not support efforts to enroll in income driven-repayment plans, and apply payments in questionable ways. CFPB recommends the development of consistent, market-wide standards that would hold student loan servicers to the same standards in place for credit cards and other consumer debt. The agency also recommends restructuring the servicer contracts so they would have strong financial incentives to serve students better.[30]

Concluding Thoughts

Prominent anecdotes about former students struggling under huge amounts of debt paint a wildly exaggerated picture of education debt in the USA. Access to credit has made it possible for millions of people—both recent high school graduates and older adults—to invest in education and training they would have missed out on if they could not borrow. The majority of borrowers owe reasonable amounts they can repay while maintaining a higher standard of living than they would have had if they had never gone to college.

Borrowing to pay for college makes sense. Our society and our economy benefit when more people are well educated and we should devote considerable public resources to ensuring that as many people as possible have access to a wide range of postsecondary options and that they have both the preparation and the resources to succeed in those endeavors. But individuals reap much of the benefit. People with postsecondary degrees and certificates earn significantly more on average than those with only a high school education. People from more affluent backgrounds are more likely to achieve higher levels of education and people with higher levels of education tend to be at the top of the income scale. They can and should pay a reasonable portion of the cost of that education. Student loans allow that payment to come out of post-college earnings.

The federal government is appropriately central to making credit available and to developing a repayment system that serves well both students, including those for whom outcomes are less favorable than anticipated, and taxpayers. The current system of federal student loans provides ample funds and includes considerable protection for borrowers facing financial difficulties, including a developing income-driven repayment system that prevents required loan payments from being unaffordable. But there is much to be done to improve the system.

Addressing the very real problems facing many former students who have borrowed requires targeting reforms to the causes of these problems. The students who struggle most are, by and large, not those with very high levels of debt. Media sensationalism aside, most—but not all—borrowers with high levels of debt have earned graduate degrees and repay their debts out of relatively high earnings. The more intractable problems are among those who borrowed small amounts of money but did not graduate. The composition of student loan borrowers has changed over time, including an increasing number of non-completers, older adults, and former for-profit sector students. In the past, these people would have been on the no-debt side of the line—and would have no postsecondary education. Addressing their problems is not the same as treating all student debt as a crisis.

Better guidance about choosing postsecondary institutions and programs and about how much and through which channels to borrow could eliminate many of the painful stories. Tighter restrictions on which institutions are eligible for federal student aid programs and on the amount of credit available to graduate students and to some undergraduates could also reduce the number of people who take loans that are likely to cause problems.

In addition to working to prevent predictably problematic borrowing, the federal government should strengthen both the protections for borrowers facing unanticipated difficulties and the bureaucratic structures surrounding the loan system. Notably, strengthening the system does not mean minimizing the amount all borrowers are required to repay. It means structuring manageable payments so borrowers meet their responsibilities with appropriate support from taxpayers.

Fixing the student loan system and the larger postsecondary financing system of which it is a part could solve some of the problems leading to the current panic about student debt, but other issues are more challenging. A better higher education financing system will not solve the problems of inadequate pre-college education, from early childhood through high school, that leaves too many people unprepared for college-level work; weak employment opportunities; growing income inequality that increases the struggles facing those not at the top of the income distribution; and a social safety net that has too many holes in it to ensure that basic needs are met for everyone—including students.

The share of the costs of postsecondary education borne by students and families directly rather than through government subsidies has increased over time without a well thought out policy agenda. It is time to rethink both how we deliver different types of education and training, with an eye to lowering costs, and how we as a society pay for this investment in the future. But those who think there is a silver bullet that can make providing high-quality education to all who can benefit from it dramatically less costly are likely to be disappointed. We must address the question of the appropriate division of the responsibility between students and taxpayers in general.

Producing high-quality education opportunities requires significant resources. Someone has to pay. Students are and should be responsible for a portion of that funding. Acknowledging that reality and working to develop a system that both prepares and protects people seeking to invest in themselves through postsecondary education should be high on the national policy agenda.

Notes

1. Kevin Carey, "Student Debt in America: Lend With a Smile, Collect With a Fist," New York Times, *The Upshot*, November 27, 2015, http://www.nytimes.com/2015/11/29/upshot/student-debt-in-america-lend-with-a-smile-collect-with-a-fist.html?_r=0.
2. Bureau of Labor Statistics, "Occupational Employment Statistics," accessed November 25, 2015, (http://www.bls.gov/oes/current/oes395012.htm).
3. U.S. Department of Education, "Three-Year Official Cohort Default Rates for Schools," Federal Student Aid, accessed November 27, 3026, http://www2.ed.gov/offices/OSFAP/defaultmanagement/cdr.html.
4. Patricia Cohen, "For-Profit Colleges Accused of Fraud Still Receive U.S. Funds," *New York Times,* October 12, 2015, http://www.nytimes.com/2015/10/13/business/for-profit-colleges-accused-of-fraud-still-receive-us-funds.html.
5. Much of the behavioral economics literature confirms the power of the "default option." See, for example, Brigitte Madrian and Dennis Shea, "The Power of Suggestion: Inertia in 401(K) Participation and Savings Behavior," *Quarterly Journal of Economics,* 116 (4:2011): 1149–1187.
6. Lamar Alexander, "Risk-Sharing/Skin-in-the Game: Concepts and Proposals," Senate Committee on Health, Education, Labor, and Pensions, March 23, 2015, https://www.insidehighered.com/sites/default/server_files/files/Risk%20Sharing2.pdf.

7. Scott Jaschik, "Bucking the Tide on Private Loans," *Inside Higher Ed*, July 16, 2007, https://www.insidehighered.com/news/2007/07/16/barnard.
8. Robert Sheets and Stephen Crawford, *From Income-based Repayment Plans to an Income-based Loan System* (Washington, DC: George Washington University, 2014), http://www.luminafoundation.org/files/publications/ideas_summit/From_Income-based_Repayment_Plans_to_an_Income-based_Loan_System.pdf.
9. Elizabeth Akers and Matthew Chingos, *Are College Students Borrowing Blindly?* Brown Center on Education Policy at Brookings, 2014, http://www.brookings.edu/~/media/research/files/reports/2014/12/10-borrowing-blindly/are-college-students-borrowing-blindly_dec-2014.pdf; Healy Whitsett, "High Debt, Low Information: A Survey of Student Loan Borrowers," NERA Economic Consulting, March 2013, http://www.nera.com/content/dam/nera/publications/archive2/PUB_Student_Loans_0312.pdf.
10. U.S. Government Accountability Office, *Federal Student Loans: Education Could Do More to Help Ensure Borrowers are Aware of Repayment and Forgiveness Options.* (Washington, DC: GAO, 2015), 15–663.
11. The new REPAYE program extends the period before forgiveness to 25 years for borrowers owing graduate school debt.
12. Some proposals for comprehensive income-driven repayment plans do not include loan forgiveness. For example, the ExCEL Act, original proposed by Rep. Tom Petri (R-WI) and reintroduced in 2015 by Reps. Jared Polis (D-Colo.) and Richard Hanna (R-N.Y.), involves payroll withholding and universal participation, but does not forgive unpaid balances.
13. Jon Queally, "The Unforgiven: How College Debt is Crushing a Generation," *Common Dreams*, November 13, 2014, http://www.commondreams.org/news/2014/11/13/unforgiven-how-college-debt-crushing-generation.
14. See Clare McCann, "Fair Value Accounting," Ed Central, 2014, http://www.edcentral.org/edcyclopedia/fair-value-accounting/.
15. http://www.nytimes.com/2014/09/13/business/student-loan-debt-burdens-more-than-just-young-people.html. In fact, $526 monthly payments would support a debt of $42,900 in a 10-year repayment plan.
16. Calculations from http://www.amortization-calc.com/.
17. Charles A. Jeszeck, *"Older Americans: Inability to Repay Student Loans May Affect Financial Security of a Small Percentage of Retirees,"* Testimony Before the Special Committee on Aging, U.S. Senate, GAO 14-866T, September 10, 2014.
18. U.S. Department of Education. "Some physical or mental impairments can qualify you for a total and permanent disability discharge on your federal student loans and/or TEACH Grant service obligation," accessed October 20, 2015, https://studentaid.ed.gov/sa/repay-loans/forgiveness-cancellation/disability-discharge.

19. Sandy Baum et al., *Trends in Students Aid 2015* (New York: The College Board, 2015).
20. Consumer Financial Protection Bureau, *Mid-year update on student loan complaints*, April 2014.
21. Betsy Mayotte, "Debunking the Student Loan Bankruptcy Myth," *U.S. News and World Report,* August 13, 2014, http://www.usnews.com/education/blogs/student-loan-ranger/2014/08/13/debunking-the-student-loan-bankruptcy-myth.
22. Michelle Ware, Evan Weissman, and Drew McDermott, *Aid Like a Paycheck: Incremental Aid to Promote Student Success* (New York: MDRC, 2013), http://www.mdrc.org/sites/default/files/ALAP%20brief.pdf paycheck#overview.
23. Alan Pyke, "Feds Fight to Make Bankrupt Man, Unemployed for a Dozen Years, Pay Back Student Loans," *Think Progress,* October 15, 2015, http://thinkprogress.org/education/2015/10/15/3712871/undue-hardship-student-loan-bankruptcy/.
24. Sandy Baum et al., *Trends in Student Aid 2015,* Figure 15.
25. See Claudia Goldin and Stephanie Cellini, "Does Federal Student Aid Raise Tuition? New Evidence on For-Profit Colleges," *American Economic Journal: Economic Policy,* 6 (November 2014): 174–206, for evidence on federal student aid driving prices up in the for-profit sector.
26. The taxation does not apply to public service loan forgiveness or other programs attached to specific occupations or for certain classes of employer. Internal Revenue Service, *Tax Benefits for Education,* Publication 970, 2014, https://www.irs.gov/publications/p970/ch05.html.
27. Suze Orman, "Attention student loan borrowers: Can you pass my repayment test?" *Suze Orman,* November 24, 2014, http://www.suzeorman.com/blog/attention-student-loan-borrowers-can-you-pass-my-repayment-test/.
28. Internal Revenue Service, "The Mortgage Forgiveness Debt Relief Act and Debt Cancellation," accessed October 23, 2015, https://www.irs.gov/Individuals/The-Mortgage-Forgiveness-Debt-Relief-Act-and-Debt-Cancellation-.
29. Sander Levin (D-MI) and Pat Tiberi (R-OH), HR 2492, May 19, 2009, https://www.congress.gov/bill/111th-congress/house-bill/2492; The White House, "Opportunity for All: Middle Class Tax Cuts in the President's FY2015 budget," Office of the Press Secretary, https://www.whitehouse.gov/the-press-office/2014/03/04/opportunity-all-middle-class-tax-cuts-president-s-fy-2015-budget.
30. Consumer Financial Protection Bureau, *Student Loan Servicing: Analysis of Public Input and Recommendations for Reform* (Washington, DC: CFPB, 2015), http://files.consumerfinance.gov/f/201509_cfpb_student-loan-servicing-report.pdf.

References

AAA Foundation for Traffic Safety. 'Road rage' on the rise. https://www.aaafoundation.org/sites/default/files/roadragePR.pdf. Accessed 20 Sept 2015.

Akers, Elizabeth. 2014. Reconsidering the conventional wisdom on student debt and home ownership. Brown Center on Education Policy at Brookings. Chalkboard. http://www.brookings.edu/research/papers/2014/05/08-student-loan-debt-and-home-ownership-akers

Akers, Elizabeth, and Matthew Chingos. 2014. *Are college students borrowing blindly?* Brown Center on Education Policy at Brookings. http://www.brookings.edu/~/media/research/files/reports/2014/12/10-borrowing-blindly/are-college-students-borrowing-blindly_dec-2014.pdf

Alexander, Lamar. 2015. Risk-sharing/Skin-in-the game: Concepts and proposals. Senate Committee on Health, Education, Labor, and Pensions. March 23. https://www.insidehighered.com/sites/default/server_files/files/Risk%20Sharing2.pdf

Allison, Melissa. 2015. Student debt has minor effect on homeownership—As long as you get a four-year degree. September 16. http://www.zillow.com/blog/student-debt-effect-homeownership-182547/

Ambrose, Brent, Larry Cordell, and Shuwei Ma. 2015. The impact of student loan debt on small business formation. July 15. SSRN: http://ssrn.com/abstract=2417676 or http://dx.doi.org/10.2139/ssrn.2417676

Anderson, Jamie. 2015. Yes, first-time buyer demand is weak. But stop blaming student debt. *Zillow Real Estate Research*. http://www.zillow.com/research/student-debt-homeownership-10563/

S. Baum, *Student Debt*, DOI 10.1057/978-1-137-52738-7

Anderson, Nick. 2015. Duncan: Colleges are falling short for millions of students. Debt-free degrees are just part of the solution. *Washington Post*, July 27. http://www.washingtonpost.com/news/grade-point/wp/2015/07/27/duncan-colleges-are-falling-short-for-millions-of-students-debt-free-degrees-are-just-part-of-the-solution/

Angrist, Joshua, Philip Oreopoulos, and Tyler Williams. 2014. When opportunity knocks, who answers? *Journal of Human Resources* 49(3): 572–610.

Avery, Christopher, and Sarah Turner. 2012. Do college students borrow too much—Or not enough? *Journal of Economic Perspectives* 26(1): 165–192.

Bartik, Timothy, Brad Hershbein, and Marta Lachowska. 2015. The effects of the Kalamazoo Promise Scholarship on college enrollment, persistence, and completion. W.E. Upjohn Institute for Employment, Research Working Paper 15-229.

Baum, Sandy. 2003. *College on credit: How borrowers perceive their education debt.* Boston: Nellie Mae.

Baum, Sandy. 2015a. *A framework for thinking about law school affordability*, The Access Group.

Baum, Sandy. 2015b. Does increasing reliance on student debt explain declines in entrepreneurial activity? The Urban Institute. http://www.urban.org/research/publication/does-increasing-reliance-student-debt-explain-declines-entrepreneurial-activity

Baum, Sandy, and Jennifer Ma. 2014. *Trends in college pricing 2014.* New York: The College Board.

Baum, Sandy, and Michael McPherson. 2011. Is education a public good or a private good? *Chronicle of Higher Education*, January 18. http://chronicle.com/blogs/innovations/is-education-a-public-good-or-a-private-good/28329

Baum, Sandy, and Diane Saunders. 1998. *Life after debt: Results of the National Student Loan Survey.* Boston: Nellie Mae.

Baum, Sandy, and Saul Schwartz. 1988. *The impact of student loans on borrowers: Consumption patterns and attitudes towards repayment.* Boston: Massachusetts Higher Education Assistance Corporation.

Baum, Sandy, Jennifer Ma, and Kathleen Payea. 2013. *Education pays: The benefits of higher education for individuals and society.* New York: The College Board.

Baum, Sandy, Jennifer Ma, and Diane Elliott. 2014. *Trends in student aid 2014.* New York: The College Board.

Baum, Sandy, Jennifer Ma, Matea Pender, and D'Wayne Bell. 2015. *Trends in student aid 2015.* New York: The College Board.

Belfield, Clive, and Thomas Bailey. 2014. The benefits of attending community college: A review of the evidence. *Community College Review* 39: 46–68.

Bernard, Tara Siegel. 2015. The many pitfalls of private student loans. *New York Times*, September 4. http://www.nytimes.com/2015/09/05/your-money/student-loans/the-many-pitfalls-of-private-student-loans.html

Bialik, Carl. 2015. Scare headlines exaggerated the U.S. crime wave. *Five Thirty-EightPolitics*,September11.http://fivethirtyeight.com/features/scare-headlines-exaggerated-the-u-s-crime-wave/

Brown, Meta and Sydnee Caldwell. 2013. Young adult student loan borrowers retreat from housing and auto markets. Federal Reserve Bank of New York. http://libertystreeteconomics.newyorkfed.org/2013/04/young-student-loan-borrowers-retreat-from-housing-and-auto-markets.html#.Vlyzs2SrRxh

Bureau of Labor Statistics. Data bases, tables, and calculators by subject. http://data.bls.gov/timeseries/LNS14000000. Accessed 15 Nov 2015.

Bureau of Labor Statistics. May 2014 National occupational employment and wage estimates United States. http://www.bls.gov/oes/current/oes_nat.htm#23-0000

Bureau of Labor Statistics. Occupational employment statistics. http://www.bls.gov/oes/current/oes395012.htm. Accessed 25 Nov 2015.

Bureau of Labor Statistics. Overview of U.S. wage data by area and occupation. http://www.bls.gov/bls/blswage.htm. Accessed 2 Nov 2015

Burton, Natasha. 2015. Stressed over student loans? 3 people share how they're paying off big debt on starter salaries. *Forbes*, August 6. http://www.forbes.com/sites/learnvest/2015/08/06/stressed-over-student-loans-3-people-share-how-theyre-paying-off-big-debt-on-star

Busteed, Brandon. 2015. Student loan debt: Major barrier to entrepreneurship. *Business Journal*, October 14. http://www.gallup.com/businessjournal/186179/student-loan-debt-major-barrier-entrepreneurship.aspx

Callis, Robert, and Melssa Kresin. 2015. Residential vacancies and homeownership in the third quarter 2015. *U.S. Census Bureau News*, October 27.

Card, David. 2001. Estimating the return to schooling: Progress on some persistent econometric problems. *Econometrica* 69(5): 1127–1160.

Carey, Kevin. 2015. Student debt in America: Lend with a smile, collect with a fist. *New York Times*, The Upshot, November 27. http://www.nytimes.com/2015/11/29/upshot/student-debt-in-america-lend-with-a-smile-collect-with-a-fist.html

Carnevale, Anthony, Ben Cheah, and Andrew Hanson. 2015. *The economic value of college majors*. Georgetown University Center on Education and the Workforce. https://cew.georgetown.edu/cew-reports/valueofcollegemajors/

Carniero, Pedro, James Heckman, and Edward Vytlacil. 2011. Estimating marginal returns to education. *American Economic Review* 101(6): 2754–2781.

Cohen, Patricia. 2015. For-profit colleges accused of fraud still receive U.S. funds. *New York Times*, October 12. http://www.nytimes.com/2015/10/13/business/for-profit-colleges-accused-of-fraud-still-receive-us-funds.html

Consumer Financial Protection Bureau. 2014. *Mid-year update on student loan complaints*. Washington, DC: CFPB. http://files.consumerfinance.gov/f/201506_cfpb_mid-year-update-on-student-loan-complaints.pdf

Consumer Financial Protection Bureau. 2015. *Student loan servicing: Analysis of public input and recommendations for reform*. Washington, DC: CFPB. http://files.consumerfinance.gov/f/201509_cfpb_student-loan-servicing-report.pdf

Davey, Monica, and Rich Smith. 2015. Murder rates rising sharply in many U.S. cities. *New York Times*, August 31. *Five Thirty Eight Politics*. http://fivethirtyeight.com/features/scare-headlines-exaggerated-the-u-s-crime-wave/

Delisle, Jason. 2014. *The graduate student debt review: The state of graduate student borrowing*. Washington: New America Education Policy Program.

Dorfman, Jeffrey. 2014. The student debt crisis is being manufactured to justify debt forgiveness. *Forbes*, July 3. http://www.forbes.com/sites/jeffreydorfman/2014/07/03/the-student-debt-crisis-is-being-manufactured-to-justify-debt-forgiveness/

Draut, Tamara. 2015. The momentum builds—Hillary Clinton releases debt-free college plan. *Demos*, August 10. http://www.demos.org/policyshop

Dunlop, Erin. 2013. *What do Stafford loans actually buy you? The effect of Stafford loan access on community college students*. CALDER Working Paper No. 94. Washington, DC: National Center for Analysis of Longitudinal Data in Education Research.

Dunne, Allison. 2014. Part five of student loan series focuses on young farmers. *WAMC*, December 19. http://wamc.org/post/part-five-student-loan-series-focuses-young-farmers

Dwyer, Rachel, Laura McCloud, and Randy Hodson. 2011. Youth debt, mastery, and self-esteem: Class-stratified effects of indebtedness on self-concept. *Social Science Research* 40(3): 727–741.

Dynarski, Susan. 2000. Hope for whom? Financial aid for the middle class and its impact on college attendance. *National Tax Journal* 53(3): 629–661.

Dynarski, Susan. 2003. Does aid matter? Measuring the effect of student aid on college attendance and completion. *American Economic Review* 93(1): 279–288.

Dynarski, Susan. 2005. *Loans, liquidity and schooling decisions*. Cambridge, MA: Harvard University.

Ebersole, John. 2015. The unexamined factors behind the student debt 'crisis'. *Forbes*, September 15. http://www.forbes.com/sites/johnebersole/2015/09/15/the-unexamined-factors-behind-the-student-debt-crisis/

Federal Reserve Bank of New York. Household credit. http://www.newyorkfed.org/regional/householdcredit.html. Accessed 25 Nov 2015.

Federal Reserve Bank of New York. 2015. *Quarterly Report on Household Debt and Credit*. https://www.newyorkfed.org/medialibrary/interactives/householdcredit/data/pdf/HHDC_2015Q3.pdf

Fry, Richard. 2014. Young adults, student debt, and economic well-being. Pew Research Center. http://www.pewsocialtrends.org/2014/05/14/young-adults-student-debt-and-economic-well-being/

Gallup and Purdue University. 2015. *Great jobs, great lives: The relationship between student debt, experiences, and perceptions of college worth.* Gallup Purdue Index 2015 Report. Washington, DC: Gallup. http://www.gallup.com/services/185888/gallup-purdue-index-report-2015.aspx

Glassner, Barry. 1999. *The culture of fear: Why Americans are afraid of the wrong things.* New York: Basic Books.

Goldin, Claudia, and Stephanie Cellini. 2014. Does federal student aid raise tuition? New evidence on for-profit colleges. *American Economic Journal: Economic Policy* 6: 174–206.

Gurgand, Marc, Adrien Lorenceau, and Thomas Mélonio. 2011. Student loans: Liquidity constraint and higher education in South Africa. Agence Française de Développement Working Paper No. 117.

Harris, Doug, and Sara Goldrick-Rab. 2012. Improving the productivity of education experiments: Lessons from a randomized study of need-based financial aid. *Educational Finance and Policy* 7(2): 143–169.

Hebel, Sara. 2014. From public good to private good: How higher education got to a tipping point. *The Chronicle of Higher Education*, March 3. http://chronicle.com/article/From-Public-Good-to-Private/145061

Heller, Donald. 2008. The impact of loans on student access. In *The effectiveness of student aid policies: What the research tells us*, ed. Sandy Baum, Michael McPherson, and Patricia Steele. New York: The College Board.

Houle, Jason, and Lawrence Berger. 2015. *The end of the American dream? Student loan debt and home ownership among young adults.* Washington, DC: Third Way. http://www.thirdway.org/report/the-end-of-the-american-dream-student-loan-debt-and-homeownership-among-young-adults

Hout, Michael. 2012. Social and economic returns to higher education in the United States. *American Review of Sociology* 38: 379–400.

Internal Revenue Service. 2014. *Tax benefits for education.* Publication 970. https://www.irs.gov/publications/p970/ch05.html

Internal Revenue Service. The Mortgage Forgiveness Debt Relief Act and debt cancellation. https://www.irs.gov/Individuals/The-Mortgage-Forgiveness-Debt-Relief-Act-and-Debt-Cancellation-. Accessed 23 Oct 2015.

Jaschik, Scott. 2007. Bucking the tide on private loans. *Inside Higher Ed,* July 16. https://www.insidehighered.com/news/2007/07/16/barnard

Jeszeck, Charles. 2014. *Older Americans: Inability to repay student loans may affect financial security of a small percentage of retirees.* GAO 14-866T. Testimony Before the Special Committee on Aging. September 10.

Johnson, Lyndon. Remarks on signing the Higher Education Act of 1965. Texas State University. http://www.txstate.edu/commonexperience/pastsite-archives/2008-2009/lbjresources/higheredact.html. Accessed 15 Oct 2015.

Kahneman, Daniel. 2011. *Thinking, fast and slow*. New York: Farrar, Straus and Giroux.

Kane, Thomas. 2007. Evaluating the impact of the D.C. Tuition assistance grant program. *Journal of Human Resources* 42(3): 555.

Kitroeff, Natalies. 2014. Young and in debt in New York City: Student loans make it hard to rent or buy a home. *New York Times*, June 6. http://www.nytimes.com/2014/06/08/realestate/student-loans-make-it-hard-to-rent-or-buy-a-home.html

Leef, George. 2012. College education is not a public good. National Association of Scholars. June 28. http://www.nas.org/articles/college_education_is_not_a_public_good

Levin, Sander (D-MI) and Pat Tiberi (R-OH), HR 2492, May 19, 2009, https://www.congress.gov/bill/111th-congress/house-bill/2492; The White House, "Opportunity for All: middle class tax cuts in the President's FY2015 budget," Office of the Press Secretary, https://www.whitehouse.gov/the-press-office/2014/03/04/opportunity-all-middle-class-tax-cuts-president-s-fy-2015-budget

Looney, Adam, and Constantine Yannelis. 2015. A crisis in student loans? How changes in the characteristics of borrowers and in the institutions they attended contributed to rising loan defaults. *Brookings Papers on Economic Activity*.

Lumina Foundation. 2015. *A benchmark for making college affordable: The rule of 10*. Indianapolis: Lumina Foundation. https://www.luminafoundation.org/files/resources/affordability-benchmark-1.pdf

Ma, Jennifer, Sandy Baum, Matea Pender, and D'Wayne Bell. 2015. *Trends in college pricing 2015*. New York: The College Board.

Madrian, Brigitte, and Dennis Shea. 2001. The power of suggestion: Inertia in 401(K) participation and savings behavior. *Quarterly Journal of Economics* 116(4): 1149–1187.

Martin, Andrew, and Andrew Lehren. 2012.A generation hobbled by the soaring cost of college. *New York Times*, May 12. http://www.nytimes.com/2012/05/13/business/student-loans-weighing-down-a-generation-with-heavy-debt.html?pagewanted=all

Matthews, Chris. 2015. Student loan debt is not hurting America's housing market. *Fortune*, July 27. http://fortune.com/2015/07/27/student-loan-debt-housing/

Mayotte, Betsy. 2014. Debunking the student loan bankruptcy myth. *U.S. News and World Report*, August 13. http://www.usnews.com/education/blogs/student-loan-ranger/2014/08/13/debunking-the-student-loan-bankruptcy-myth

McCann, Clare. 2014. Fair value accounting. Ed Central. http://www.edcentral.org/edcyclopedia/fair-value-accounting/.

Mishory, Jen, and Rory O'Sullivan. 2012. *The student perspective on federal financial aid reform*. Washington, DC: Young Invincibles.

Moore, Peter. 2015. Three-fifths want taxes to fund debt-free college. YouGov. August 20. https://today.yougov.com/news/2015/08/20/three-fifths-want-debt-free-college/

Moretti, Enrico. 2004. Estimating the social return to higher education: Evidence from longitudinal and repeated cross-sectional data. *Journal of Econometrics* 12: 175–212. http://eml.berkeley.edu/~moretti/socret.pdf.

NCES. 2015. *Digest of education statistics 2014.* Washington, DC: U.S. Department of Education.

NCES. National Postsecondary Student Aid Study 2012. PowerStats. http://nces.ed.gov/datalab/

O'Malley, Martin. 2015. Federal solutions to our student loan problem. *Washington Post,* April 23. https://www.washingtonpost.com/opinions/federal-solutions-to-our-student-loan-problem/2

Oreopoulos, Philip, and Uros Petronijevic. 2013. Making college worth it: A review of the returns to higher education. *The Future of Children* 23(1): 41–64.

Ormon, Suze. 2014. Attention student loan borrowers: Can you pass my repayment test?" Suze Orman blog. November 24. http://www.suzeorman.com/blog/attention-student-loan-borrowers-can-you-pass-my-repayment-test/

Patel, Reshma, Lashawn Richburg-Hayes, Elijah de la Campa, and Timothy Rudd. 2013. *Performance-based scholarships: What have we learned?* MDRC Policy Brief. New York: MDRC.

Popper, Nathaniel. 2015. Stolen consumer data is a smaller program than it seems. *New York Times,* The Upshot. August 2. http://www.nytimes.com/2015/08/02/business/stolen-consumer-data-is-a-smaller-problem-than-it-seems.html?_r=0&abt=0002&abg=1

Progressive Change Campaign Committee. Sign the petition for debt-free college. http://act.boldprogressives.org/survey/survey_freecollege/#ProgressiveBudget. Accessed 15 Oct 2015.

Pyke, Alan. 2015. Feds fight to make bankrupt man, unemployed for a dozen years, pay back student loans. *Think Progress,* October 15. http://thinkprogress.org/education/2015/10/15/3712871/undue-hardship-student-loan-bankruptcy/

Queally, Jon. 2014. The unforgiven: How college debt is crushing a generation. *Common Dreams*, November 13. http://www.commondreams.org/news/2014/11/13/unforgiven-how-college-debt-crushing-generation

Radwin, David, Jennifer Wine, Peter Siegel, and Michael Bryan. 2013. *2011-12 National Postsecondary Student Aid Study (NPSAS:12): Student financial aid estimates for 2011-12.* NCES 2013-165. Washington, DC: National Center for Education Statistics.

Rampell, Catherine. 2014. Higher education went from being a public good to a private one. *Washington Post*, May 22. http://www.washingtonpost.com/opinions/catherine-rampell-higher-education-went-from-being-a-public-good-to-a-private-one/2014/05/22/50263a16-e1bd-11e3-9743-bb9b59cde7b9_story.html

Saad, Lydia. 2014. Ebola ranks among Americans' top three health concerns. *Gallup,* November 17. http://www.gallup.com/poll/179429/ebola-ranks-among-americans-top-three-healthcare-concerns.aspx

Schneider, Mark. 2013. Higher education pays: But a lot more for some graduates than for others. *American Institutes for Research.* .http://www.air.org/resource/higher-education-pays-lot-more-some-graduates-others

Seitz-Wald, Adam. 2015. Clinton's sweeping new debt-free college plan. *MSNBC,* August10.http://www.msnbc.com/msnbc/clintons-sweeping-new-debt-free-college-plan

Shane, Scott. 2015. Is student debt the reason millennials aren't starting companies? *Entrepreneur*, August 3. http://www.entrepreneur.com/article/249036

Shapiro, Doug, Afet Dundar, Mary Ziskin, Xin Yuan, and Autumn Harrell. 2014. *Completing College: A National View of Student Attainment Rates – Fall 2008 Cohort.* Signature Report No. 8. Herndon, VA: National Student Clearinghouse Research Center.

Sheets, Robert, and Stephen Crawford. 2014. *From income-based repayment plans to an income-based loan system.* Washington, DC: George Washington University. http://www.luminafoundation.org/files/publications/ideas_summit/From_Income-based_Repayment_Plans_to_an_Income-based_Loan_System.pdf

Shoenberger, Chana. 2015. Want to be an entrepreneur? Beware of student debt. *Wall Street Journal*, May 26. http://www.wsj.com/articles/want-to-be-an-entrepreneur-beware-of-student-debt-1432318500

Skinner, Curtis, and Valerie Panne. 2015. Students across U.S. march over debt, free public college. *Reuters*, November 12. http://www.reuters.com/article/2015/11/13/us-usa-college-protests-idUSKCN0T116W20151113#K4RfqD6rxHkPC4qY.97

Solis, Alex. Credit access and college enrollment. Paper presented at the 2015 meeting of the American Economic Association, Boston. https://www.aeaweb.org/aea/2015conference/program/retrieve.php?pdfid=862

Statistic Brain Research Institute. Home foreclosure statistics. http://www.statisticbrain.com/home-foreclosure-statistics/. Accessed 2 Nov 2015

Stratford, Michael. 2015a. Debt-free and (Mostly) detail-free. *Inside Higher Ed*, June 19. https://www.insidehighered.com/news/2015/06/19/debt-free-movement-colleges-see-challenges-and-opportunities-few-details

Stratford, Michael. 2015b. Debt-free catches on. *Inside Higher Ed,* May 11. https://www.insidehighered.com/news/2015/05/11/push-liberals-debt-free-college-gains-traction-2016-democratic-campaign

The Daily Show With Jon Stewart. October 18, 2011. http://www.cc.com/video-clips/5510me/the-daily-show-with-jon-stewart-occupy-wall-street-divided/;November16,2011.http://www.cc.com/video-clips/409tf3/the-daily-show-with-jon-stewart-the-99-

The White House. 2014. Opportunity for all: Middle class tax cuts in the President's FY2015 budget. Office of the Press Secretary, March 4. https://www.whitehouse.gov/the-press-office/2014/03/04/opportunity-all-middle-class-tax-cuts-president-s-fy-2015-budget

Think Tank. 2015. Comment on Darian Woods, "Medicine, law, business: Which grad students borrow the most?" *NPR Planet Money,* July 16. http://www.npr.org/sections/money/2015/07/15/422590257/medicine-law-business-which-grad-students-borrow-the-most

Tiberi, Pat, and Sander Levin. 2009. HR 2492. May 19. https://www.congress.gov/bill/111th-congress/house-bill/2492

U.S. Census Bureau. 2014. *Current population survey.* Annual Social and Economic Supplement, Educational Attainment. http://www.census.gov/hhes/socdemo/education/data/cps/2014/tables.html

U.S. Census Bureau. 2015. *Current population survey.* Annual Social and Economic Supplement, PINC-03. https://www.census.gov/hhes/www/cpstables/032015/perinc/toc.htm

U.S. Department of Education. 2015a. Aid recipients summary. Federal Student Aid. https://studentaid.ed.gov/sa/about/data-center/student/title-iv

U.S. Department of Education. 2015b. National student loan default rates. Federal Student Aid. http://www.ifap.ed.gov/eannouncements/attachments/093015AttachOfficialFY20123YRCDRBriefing.pdf

U.S. Department of Education. 2015c. Three-year official Cohort default rates for schools. Federal Student Aid. http://www2.ed.gov/offices/OSFAP/defaultmanagement/cdr.html

U.S. Department of Education. Some physical or mental impairments can qualify you for a total and permanent disability discharge *on* your federal student loans *and/or TEACH* Grant service obligation. https://studentaid.ed.gov/sa/repay-loans/forgiveness-cancellation/disability-discharge. Accessed 20 Oct 2015.

U.S. Department of Education. College scorecard. https://collegescorecard.ed.gov/. Accessed 15 Nov 2015.

U.S. Government Accountability Office. 2015. *Federal student loans: Education could do more to help ensure borrowers are aware of repayment and forgiveness options.* 15-663. Washington, DC: GAO.

U.S. House of Representatives. H.Res.214. http://www.gpo.gov/fdsys/pkg/BILLS-114hres214ih/pdf/BILLS-114hres214ih.pdf. Accessed 2 Nov 2015.

USLegal.com. Age of majority. http://minors.uslegal.com/age-of-majority/

Vespa, Jonathan, Jamie Lewis, and Rose Kreider. 2013. *America's families and living arrangements, 2012.* P20-570. Washington, DC: U.S. Census Bureau.

Walsh, Ben. 2014. The one argument in favor of student loans. *Huffington Post,* October 2. http://www.huffingtonpost.com/2014/10/02/student-loan-benefits_n_5916512.html

Ware, Michelle, Evan Weissman, and Drew McDermott. 2013. *Aid like a paycheck: Incremental aid to promote student success.* New York: MDRC.

Warren, Elizabeth. The affordability crisis: Rescuing the dream of college education for the working class and poor. Shanker Institute and the American Federation of Teachers. http://www.warren.senate.gov/files/documents/ / ShankerInstitute-AFTEducationSpeech.pdf. Accessed 10 Nov 2015.

Whitsett, Healy. 2013. High debt, low information: A survey of student loan borrowers. Philadelphia: NERA Economic Consulting, March 21. http://www.nera.com/content/dam/nera/publications/archive2/PUB_Student_Loans_0312.pdf

Wiederspan, Mark. Denying loan access: The student-level consequences when community colleges opt out of the Stafford Loan Program. *Economics of Education Review*. Forthcoming.

Wikipedia. Moral panic. https://en.wikipedia.org/wiki/Moral_panic. Accessed 10 Nov 2015.

Willard, Lucas. 2014. Part Seven of student loan series: Sticker shock. *WAMC*, December 22. http://wamc.org/post/part-seven-student-loan-series-sticker-shock

Young Invincibles. 2015. *A higher education promise for the 21st century*. Washington, DC: Young Invincibles. http://younginvincibles.org/wp-content/uploads/2015/06/YI-Higher-Ed-Agenda.pdf

Zarembo, Alan. 2015. Generous GI bill isn't keeping today's veterans out of student loan debt. *Los Angeles Times*, October 30. http://www.latimes.com/nation/la-na-veteran-debt-20151031-story.html

Zimmerman, Bill. 2014. How to save the victims of the student loan crisis. *Huffington Post*, April 14. http://www.huffingtonpost.com/bill-zimmerman/how-to-save-the-victims-o_b_4776528.html

Zornick, George. 2015. Hillary Clinton joins debt-free college push with a big plan. *The Nation*, August 11. http://www.thenation.com/article/hillary-clinton-joins-debt-free-college-push-with-a-big-plan/

Index

A

Alternatives to borrowing, 65, 68–9, 78
American Opportunity Tax Credit (AOTC), 34
annual borrowing, 18, 22
appropriations, 51, 67
associate degree recipients, 26, 30, 75, 100
availability cascade, 45

B

bachelor's degree recipients, 2–4, 7, 13, 25, 28, 29, 57, 59, 71
bankruptcy, 94, 96–9
Barnard College, 90
Bergeron, David, 47
borrowing, a reasonable option, 6, 46, 54, 102
borrowing by sector, 9, 10, 22, 25–6, 29, 39

C

causation and correlation, 67, 72, 76–7
Center for American Progress, 47
Clinton, Hillary, 48
college prices, 5, 31–4
college scorecard, 58
college student demographics, 9
completion, 9, 28, 29, 39
Consumer Financial Protection Bureau (CFPB), 97, 102
Crawford, Steven, 90
credit card debt, 5, 64n45, 72, 96, 98

D

daily show, 8
debt by degree type, 4, 25–7
debt-free college, 5, 46–8
debt levels, older students, 28–30

S. Baum, *Student Debt*, DOI 10.1057/978-1-137-52738-7

default, 10, 12, 13, 21, 28, 36–40, 59, 67, 86, 87, 97
demos, 48
Direct Loan Program, 18
Duncan, Arne, 48

E

earnings, college graduates, 26, 27, 56–8
earnings premium, 7, 56–8
education tax credits, 33
efficiency, 50
entrepreneurship, 72, 73
equity, 5, 19, 34, 50, 66, 99
equity and efficiency, 19, 50
externalities, 53

F

family income, 9, 34, 71
Federal Reserve Bank of New York, 21, 22, 24, 37, 39, 74
Five Thirty-Eight Politics, 44
forgiving outstanding student debt, 5, 6, 21, 84, 93–4, 99
for-profit colleges, 9, 10, 12, 13, 22, 25–6, 29–30, 38–9, 84, 87, 100

G

Gainful Employment, 88
Gallup poll, 45
Gallup-Purdue poll, 76
Glassner, Barry, 45
graduate student borrowing, 7, 10–2, 23, 89
graduate student debt, 3, 6, 15, 27–8
graduate tax, 20
Great Recession, 22, 66, 89
Guaranteed Student Loan Program, 17
guidance, 6, 12, 60, 86, 88, 89, 103

H

Hebel, Sarah, 52, 62n30
Higher Education Act, 17, 49
higher taxes, 68, 69, 73
home ownership, 11, 47, 56, 66, 73–7
human capital, 56

I

impact of student debt, 47, 65–81
income distribution of borrowers, 7, 8
income-driven repayment, 2, 3, 28, 37, 91–2, 94, 96–8, 101, 103
independent students, 100
inequality, 34–6, 38, 50, 89
information, 40, 44, 57, 58, 74, 76, 90, 91, 94
interest rates, 6, 18, 20, 21, 46, 59, 90, 94–7

J

Johnson, Lyndon, 49
JP Morgan, 44

K

Kahneman, Daniel, 45

L

law student debt, 27
liquidity, 19, 49, 59, 85
living expenses, 4, 32–3, 46, 48, 99
loan limits, 18, 84, 89, 99–101
loan servicing, 101–2
loans, impact on access, 5, 49–50
loan subsidies, 4–5
lowering interest rates, 6, 21, 46, 94–5
Lumina Foundation, 57

M
Master's degree recipts, 27
Middle Income Student Assistance Program, 18
Million Student March, 5
Mitchell, Ted, 47
moral panic, 45
mortgage crisis, 11

N
National Defense Student Loan Program, 17
need-based aid, 49, 89
net prices, 33, 68, 100
New York University (NYU), 9
non-completion, 13, 40, 59, 86
Nova Southeastern, 10

O
Occupy Wall Street, 7
older students, 28–30, 59, 86
O'Malley, Martin, 47
outstanding student debt, 5–10, 21, 22, 24, 60–7, 93

P
parental resources, 71
Pell Grants, 34, 87
perceptions and evidence, 76–7
per-student borrowing, 23
Pew Research Center, 71
PLUS= loans, 18, 27, 99
Post-9/11 GI bill, 32
postsecondary enrollment, 9, 30, 50
preventing excessive borrowing, 3, 7, 27, 91
private loans, 21, 90, 97
progressive change campaign committee, 46
public benefits, 52–4
public goods, 52–4
public policy, 48, 78, 83–106
public subsidies, 46, 49, 50, 53, 78, 86
public subsidies for students, motivation, 19–21

R
Rampell, Catherine, 52
Rothstein, Jesse, 78
Rouse, Ceceila, 78

S
Sallie Mae, 17, 97
Sheets, Robert, 90
social security, 69, 94, 96–7
Stafford loans, 18, 23, 27, 62n28
Starting businesses, 7, 56, 71–3, 76, 77
state aid policies, 31
state funding, 51
student debt anecdotes, 1–4, 5
student loan crisis, 4–7
student loans, federal role, 6, 12, 17, 19–21, 49, 102
student loans, history, 17–18

T
Target, 44
taxes, 2, 52, 54, 68, 74, 78
total annual borrowing, 22–3
tuition, 5, 6, 18, 19, 26, 27, 31–4, 46, 48, 51, 54, 55, 66, 67, 69, 76, 84, 89, 98–100
tuition by state, 30–1

U
uncertainty, 7, 57, 58
underborrowing, 50

unemployment, 34, 66, 84
University of Phoenix, 10
unpaid interest, 36, 95–6

V
variation in outcomes, 17, 20, 58, 70, 91
veterans, 32, 40n1

W
Walden University, 10
Warren, Elizabeth, 48, 94
withholding, 92, 93

Y
Young Invincibles, 47, 61n16